P9-CKA-022

Martha Stewart's
FRUIT DESSERTS

Sour Cherry Pie,
page 193

Martha Stewart's
FRUIT
DESSERTS

100+ Delicious Ways to Savor the Best of Every Season

From the Kitchens of Martha Stewart

Photographs by Johnny Miller and Others

Clarkson Potter/Publishers
New York

Copyright © 2021 by
Martha Stewart Living Omnimedia, LP
All rights reserved.

Published in the United States by Clarkson Potter/
Publishers, an imprint of Random House,
a division of Penguin Random House LLC, New York.
clarksonpotter.com
marthastewart.com

CLARKSON POTTER is a trademark and
POTTER with colophon is a registered trademark
of Penguin Random House LLC.

Library of Congress Cataloging-in-Publication Data
Names: Miller, Johnny, other. |
Martha Stewart Living Omnimedia, author.
Title: Martha Stewart's Fruit Desserts:
100+ delicious ways to savor the best of every season /
from the kitchens of Martha Stewart Living.
Description: First edition. | New York:
Clarkson Potter/Publishers, [2021] | Includes index.
Identifiers: LCCN 2020050766 (print) |
LCCN 2020050767 (ebook) |
ISBN 9780593139189 (hardcover) |
ISBN 9780593139196 (ebook)
Subjects: LCSH: Desserts. | Cooking (Fruit) |
LCGFT: Cookbooks.
Classification: LCC TX773 .M2688 2021 (print) |
LCC TX773 (ebook) | DDC 641.86—DC23
LC record available at https://lccn.loc.gov/2020050766
LC ebook record available at
https://lccn.loc.gov/2020050767

ISBN 978-0-593-13918-9
Ebook ISBN 978-0-593-13919-6

Printed in China

Cover design by Michael McCormick

Cover photographs by Johnny Miller

See page 248 for a complete
list of photography credits.

10 9 8 7 6 5 4 3 2 1

First edition

To all the farmers and orchard growers
who grow amazing varieties
of fruits, providing us, the consumers and
cooks and bakers, with the most
delicious ingredients for the recipes
we developed for this book

Blueberry Pie with Lattice-
Weave Crust, page 170

Deep-Dish Dried-Apple and
Cranberry Pie, page 96

CONTENTS

SPRING

SUMMER

The Basics

Acknowledgments and Photo Credits

Index

Peach-Cardamom
Upside-Down Cake,
page 173

Citrus Flan, page 91

FROM MARTHA

One of life's great pleasures is biting into a perfect apple, a juicy peach, or a sweet-tart plum. Transforming those tender stone fruits, sour lemons, meaty, fragrant pumpkins, or a few cups of ripe berries into a pie or galette, or a delectable cake, is yet another way to enjoy the fruits of America's extraordinary growers. Over the thirty years we have been creating recipes for our magazine *Martha Stewart Living*, we have developed, baked, and photographed hundreds of desserts that focus on fruit as a main ingredient. These recipes are consistently readers' favorites and have been well used by them for many different occasions. We hope you will adore this collection, arranged by season, and add many of the recipes to your personal repertoire.

I have been baking for a long time. In fact, baking is what I most enjoy when preparing food. I like measuring, I like chemistry, I like the mechanics of stand mixers and food processors and use them when I can. I love watching a cake rise in the oven and a piecrust brown to just the perfect golden shade. The addition of fruits like berries and citrus to batters and fillings contributes even more excitement—and that is what this book is all about!

As a child, we grew certain things in our suburban garden—apples, peaches, and lots of berries, even rhubarb. Mom would use every last scrap of each in the myriad pies and desserts we were treated to each day. Our baker neighbors, Mr. and Mrs. Maus (they had retired from their own bakery), taught me many baking tricks and tips about mixing, folding, and cutting that few books at the time revealed. Childhood was indeed the best introduction for a home cook like me, who was curious and willing to take the time to make from scratch.

On summer trips to the Jersey shore, we stopped the car at farm stands to purchase quarts of blueberries—in my mind, the best in the nation—or pecks of white peaches for ice cream or tarts. On family outings to Long Island, we bought ripe strawberries in June and pie pumpkins in the fall. At that time, we did not have the farmers' markets that are now in almost every county but had to look in many places for great fruits to incorporate into our baking.

This book is your guide, your primer, your inspiration for utilizing all the amazing fruits that are at your fingertips, and I hope you and your families will savor every bite.

Martha Stewart

GOLDEN RULES

1. Bake in season: Depending on where you live, the peak seasons for fruits vary; but use the Essential Ingredients on pages 14 through 16 as a guide. For the freshest picks, look to nearby orchards, your local farmers' market, or maybe even your own backyard. Choose what looks good that day and don't hesitate to discover new, interesting cultivars. Before baking, be sure to taste the fruit. Factors like ripeness, seasonality, and variety can dramatically affect sweetness. Adjust the sugar accordingly, adding a little less if, say, the berries are delightfully sweet, more if they're tart. The fruit, after all, is the featured ingredient.

2. Prep before you begin: Read the recipe all the way through, setting out ingredients like butter and eggs that need to be room temperature, allowing time for dough to chill (you can even make the dough ahead, refrigerating it up to 2 days or freezing it up to 3 months; thawing pastry in the refrigerator the night before). Gather your essential tools—rolling pin, bowls, pan—and prepare (peel, chop, measure) all ingredients at the start. A proper mise en place will ensure an efficient process.

3. Use quality ingredients: Use in-season fruit and fresh eggs, opting for organic when you can. We prefer unsalted butter to control the salt in a recipe; unbleached flour when using all-purpose, as it provides more structure than softer, bleached flour; and kosher salt—like Diamond Crystal—as table salt is saltier by measure.

4. Don't waste: When rolling out dough for pastry, there are often little pieces that don't get used. Save those scraps. Reroll and cut them into shapes to decorate your dessert, or to serve alongside. Or simply butter, sprinkle with sugar, and bake them up for teatime snacks. You can even freeze them until you have enough to make a whole new pastry crust. If you have extra frangipane, add it to the weekend's French toast. Drizzle any extra poaching liquid into cocktails or over ice cream. Use that discarded vanilla bean to make vanilla sugar. And always keep a bowl near your workspace to collect produce scraps for the compost.

5. Know your oven: Every oven is different and may vary from the set temperature, so it helps to use a thermometer for accuracy and to learn your oven's hot spots. Most ovens have heat sources in the top and bottom. In general, place items on the upper rack to achieve a crispy top, middle rack for even air circulation, and lower rack for the bottom to be browned nicely. Many of the recipes in this book make recommendations for optimal rack placement, sometimes also suggesting a lined baking sheet on a lower rack to catch any juices.

6. Learn to trust your baking instincts: Follow the guidelines in the recipe and pay attention to visual cues, smells, and tastes. Notice the color to help identify doneness: Many pies and tarts are done when the crust is a lovely golden brown, but you can't rely on that alone, as sometimes browning happens too quickly (if so, you can tent them with foil). Look also for signs that the filling is done—fruit should be bubbling, indicating that the starch has been activated, which will produce a deliciously thick, not watery, texture. You should also notice rich aromas, like vanilla, spices, and fruit.

ESSENTIAL INGREDIENTS: FRUIT 101

AUTUMN

Apples: Synonymous with fall, apples come in so many delightful varieties, some that are better for snacking than baking. Apples that hold up well to baking include Golden Delicious, Fuji, Mutsu, Honeycrisp, Rome, Macoun, Jonathan, and Pink Lady. They should be fragrant, firm, brightly colored, and free of bruises or soft spots. If using within a few days, leave them at room temperature; otherwise, store in the refrigerator, and wash just before using.

Cranberries: These tart jewels are available October through December. Ripe cranberries are deep red and very firm. Before using, rinse in a bowl of cold water (the berries will float, thanks to a pocket of air that also allows them to bounce) and discard any unripe, bruised, shriveled, or broken ones. They freeze well–up to a year–and can often be cooked without defrosting.

Figs: With their delicate skin, floral sweetness, and lush texture, fresh figs are available summer through fall. Select plump figs, avoiding mushy ones. They're highly perishable, so use them immediately or refrigerate for up to two days. Common varieties include the purple–black Mission and the pale green Calimyrna.

Grapes: Available as early as May and deep into fall, grapes are nature's candy. They should be plump, with smooth unbroken skins, and stems firmly attached. Often, they are covered with a whitish bloom, a natural protection against moisture loss and spoilage. Store grapes in the refrigerator up to a week and rinse just before using. They come in green (try Thompson and Muscat varieties, used for making wine and raisins); blue–black (such as Zante, used to make dried currants, and Concord, used in jams, jellies, and sorbets); as well as red (Red Flame and Crimson are good for baking).

Pears: These alluring fruits arrive as early as August and are available through winter. Choose firm specimens. Most varieties are harvested when mature but not ripe, so they typically need two to four days at cool room temperature to become soft and fragrant. A pear matures from the inside out, so check for ripeness at the thinner stem end–the flesh should yield to pressure. Baking pears include Anjou, Bartlett, and Bosc. Anjou and Bosc are ideal for broiling and poaching, too (for how-to, see page 244). Their crunchy, dense texture holds up well under heat, and their sweet-spicy flavor is strong enough that it won't be overpowered by other ingredients in recipes. Comice pears are very sweet and juicy; cook them when slightly underripe so they don't add too much moisture to the dish.

Quinces: Look for this charmingly misshapen, rich-yellow fruit in late fall. Strikingly sour when raw, quince shines when cooked. Heat it gently to allow the flesh to soften and release its honeyed sweetness. Cooked quince retains its shape nicely, taking on a tawny pink hue and a flavor mildly reminiscent of spiced apple and guava. Store the fresh fruit at room temperature up to a week and in the refrigerator up to three weeks.

WINTER

Bananas: Available year-round, this snacking standby is a wonderful winter baking fruit. Look for bright yellow bananas to eat right away or green to ripen at home. They should be firm and free of bruises, with stems intact. Store at room temperature. To ripen faster, place them in a paper bag with an apple. Bananas can be frozen, peeled and sealed in a plastic bag, up to two months.

Lemons: When choosing this lip-puckering citrus, look for firm, glossy, bright yellow, and thin-skinned fruits that feel heavy for their size. Avoid any that are too soft or too hard. If using within the next few days, leave it out at room temperature. Otherwise, refrigerate in the crisper for up to several weeks. If you have extra lemons, grate the zest and squeeze the juice. Freeze zest in resealable freezer bags and the juice in ice-cube trays; when solid, transfer the cubes to resealable freezer bags and keep frozen up to three months. Meyer lemons are a particular favorite of Martha's.

Limes: The Persian variety of this tart green citrus is most common, and available year-round. The limes are harvested when deep green and not fully ripe, for maximum flavor and acidity. Choose those that are heavy for their size, with smooth skin and no brown spots. Key limes, which have been grown in the Florida Keys since the 1500s, are less common in stores and tend to be pricier. Small and yellowish, they are full of flavor and have a distinctive aroma, so while the little gems provide less juice than their Persian counterpart, they are worth the effort.

Oranges: Though you can buy them year-round, oranges are best in winter. Look for fruits that are smooth-skinned, firm, and heavy for its size. Color is not necessarily an indication of quality, as even ripe oranges can have traces of green. Keep oranges in a cool spot for up to a week or in the refrigerator for up to two weeks. When zesting, remove only the pigmented outer layer of skin, avoiding the bitter white pith underneath.

Passion fruits: Native to Brazil, this fruit was named by early missionaries who saw all the elements of Christ's passion depicted in its flowers. Inside its wrinkly (inedible) purple skin, you'll find small black seeds in a fragrant yellow pulp.

Pineapples: Though its peak harvest is March through July, pineapple is available year-round and certainly brightens up winter. Look for fruits that are fragrant, yield when you squeeze, and are heavy for their size. Avoid any with soft spots (overripe) or a greenish tint at either end (underripe). The leaves should be green and look fresh. Store whole, uncut at room temperature up to two days or in the refrigerator up to three days. To cut, chop off the top and bottom, stand it on its end, and slice off the skin from top to bottom using a large, sharp knife. Scoop out the eyes. Slice the flesh, cut away the core, and continue slicing as the recipe directs or as desired.

Pomegranates: Cultivated since ancient times, pomegranates are the stuff of folklore. In the northern hemisphere, they are available in fall through February. The fruit's jewel-like red arils (often referred to as seeds) are the edible parts, and they hold bursts of sweet-tart juice. Choose pomegranates that are heavy for their size. Cut the fruit horizontally, hold one half over a bowl, cut-side down, and hit the top and sides with a heavy spoon until the fruit softens and releases its seeds. Refrigerate the seeds in an airtight container for up to two weeks.

SPRING

Mangoes: Peak season is March through July, but nowadays mangoes are available year-round. They can be enjoyed when ripe and sweet or unripe ("green") and tart. For the former, choose mangoes that are plump, yield to gentle pressure, and have a sweet scent at the stem end; they will ripen further if kept at room temperature for a few days. Once ripe, refrigerate for up to three days. To eat, stand a mango on end and cut off its "cheeks," drawing a knife along the contour of the seed. There are more than five hundred varieties, but a favorite is Champagne.

Rhubarb: Technically a vegetable and not a fruit, rhubarb is included here because it is commonly baked with fruit. Rhubarb's long, thick stalks range in color from deep red to pinkish tinged with green. There are two main types: hothouse, grown indoors and sold year-round, and field-grown, which has a bit more flavor and is available from April to July. Choose crisp stalks that are about an inch wide, with no brown spots. Refrigerate, in a plastic bag, for up to one week. Because it's very tart, rhubarb is almost always cooked with sugar and often combined with red fruits, such as strawberries or raspberries. To prepare, rinse

(continued)

well, then trim the bottoms and tops. If there are any leaves, slice off and discard them (they are toxic). If the stalks are stringy, remove strings with a paring knife.

Strawberries: For the best-tasting strawberries, look for locally grown ones that are brightly colored, sweet-smelling, and plump, with no white or green around the stem. Smaller berries tend to have more flavor, as larger ones contain more water. Avoid soft, shriveled, or bruised fruits, and check for mold. Do not rinse or hull fruits until you are ready to use them. If not using right away, refrigerate up to three days.

SUMMER

Apricots: If you only know this little stone fruit in dried form, you're in for a treat. Fresh, ripe apricots are juicy, tender, and both sweet and tart. Look for them from May through August. For the best flavor, try to seek out local fruit, and choose those that are deep orange, fairly plump, and soft enough to yield to gentle pressure (but not mushy). Place unripe apricots in a paper bag at room temperature for one to two days. Fully ripe should be used immediately; otherwise, refrigerate for up to one week.

Berries: Depending upon the local climate, blueberries, raspberries, and blackberries are best mid-summer to early fall. Wild berries are smaller and more intensely flavored than cultivated, which are available year-round. In general, choose berries that are plump and vibrant. (In addition to the widely available red raspberry, look for black and yellow varieties—Martha grows all three.) Discard any that are moldy or leaking their juices. Avoid stained or damp packages, as the fruit inside may be spoiled. Refrigerate them in the original container up to five days. When you're ready to bake, rinse berries under cold water, drain, and pat dry.

Cherries: Start looking for bright, plump, and firm cherries, with stems intact, as early as May. Store them, unwashed, in the refrigerator, for up to five days. A cherry pitter helps remove pits easily; otherwise, make a cut around each fruit with a paring knife, as you would to pit a peach. Martha is a big fan of sour cherries, like Montmorency and Morello, for baking. Smaller and tarter than your average Bing or golden Rainier (sweet varieties you want for eating fresh, out of hand), these rare beauties have a fleeting season of a couple weeks from June to July, depending on where you live. Look for them at farmers' markets.

Melons: For honeydew and cantaloupe, choose fruits that are fragrant and have a cream or golden (not green) rind. Avoid those with soft spots, although the end opposite the stem should be slightly soft. Watermelon should be heavy, firm, and sound hollow when thumped. A properly ripened watermelon should have a yellow spot on one side, where it sat on the ground.

Nectarines: Like smaller, sweeter, smoother (no fuzz in sight) peaches, nectarines are a spring through late-summer delight. Choose fragrant specimens that have a slight give when pressed and avoid those with marks. Store nectarines on the counter. To help ripen, slip into a paper bag for a day or two.

Peaches: Prime time is late June through August. Choose fruit with a fragrant aroma and flesh that yields a bit when pressed. Don't buy a peach if it has cuts or spots, or if it's rock-hard or mushy. Color has more to do with variety than ripeness; but those that are tinged with green are usually underripe. For the best flavor, look for locally grown, tree-ripened peaches. To ripen at home, place in a paper bag with an apple or banana at room temperature. Store ripe peaches in the refrigerator for up to five days; allow them to sit at room temperature before eating.

Plums: One of the earliest cultivated fruits, plums are as varied as they are delicious. In season May through October, domestic plums are crimson to black-red with a yellow or reddish flesh. European varieties, which peak in fall, are green, blue, or purple and have a golden-yellow flesh. Look for plums that are plump, yielding gently to pressure. Avoid any with wrinkled or broken skin or extremely soft spots. Ripen plums in a paper bag at room temperature for one to two days. Once ripe, refrigerate up to three days.

ESSENTIAL TOOLS

Pie pan, check. Rolling pin, check. What else does a baker need?
Stock your workspace with these key pieces and set yourself up for success.

Mixing bowls: A set of heatproof glass bowls are indispensable, whether you need to organize mise en place, whisk ingredients, or improvise for a double boiler.

Whisk: Choose a sturdy stainless-steel variety that feels nicely weighted in your hand.

Measuring cups: Spoon dry ingredients, like flour and sugar, and semisolid ones, like sour cream, into nesting cups; use a straight edge to level off the ingredients. Pour liquid ingredients into a heatproof glass measuring cup, checking for accuracy at eye level.

Measuring spoons: Choose a graduated set of spoons with deep wells, so ingredients don't spill out.

Sieve: Use a fine-mesh sieve to sift ingredients, like flour or confectioners' sugar—removing any lumps—or to strain fruit purée.

Offset spatulas: The blade and angled design lifts your grip, allowing you to stay out of your own way while you bake. Use a small offset spatula to spread batter evenly and smoothly. Use a large offset spatula to frost a cake.

Flexible spatula: Silicone spatulas are heatproof, won't pick up flavors, and are safe to use on nonstick pans. Use them to fold in ingredients or to transfer batters from bowl to pan.

Rimmed baking sheet: Heavy-duty pure aluminum half sheets, with one-inch-high rims and rolled edges, don't buckle and they conduct heat, ensuring even baking.

Bench scraper: Rely on this multipurpose tool to divide dough into portions, loosen it from a work surface, transfer cut-up ingredients to a bowl, or even slide trimmings into the compost.

Ruler: Keep a 12-inch ruler nearby to measure dough when rolling.

Paring knife and peeler: If well-made and sharp, this pair is all you really need to prep fruit. To process a large quantity quickly, you might also want a mandoline and an apple corer.

Kitchen shears: Reach for these whenever you need to cut parchment or trim pastry dough. The blades can separate for easy washing.

Microplane: The supersharp teeth finely grate everything from citrus peel to chocolate.

Pastry brush: Keep two brushes—a wet one for applying butter and egg wash, and a dry one for sweeping away excess flour.

Piping bag: Have a reusable pastry bag with basic tips on hand for piping meringue, pâte à choux, frosting, or whipped cream.

Oven thermometer: This is your insurance against unreliable oven temperatures.

Mixing bowls, whisk, measuring cups and spoons, sieve, flexible spatula, Microplane, and piping bag with tips, all Martha Stewart Collection created for Macy's

AUTUMN

Harvest season brings crisp air and bustling life
to orchards and farm stands. Ripe, mellow fruits are abundant.
Carry them home by the armful to enhance with warm
spices and cook to bubbling under flaky crusts
of pies, pandowdies, crostatas, and grunts.

PINK-APPLE TART

Calvados, a French apple brandy, gives this pretty pink tart a pleasing kick. It goes into the buttery applesauce filling—watch those bubbles when you add it to the pan!—and into the red currant jelly glaze that you brush over the fruit and pastry after baking. **SERVES 12**

1 disk Pâte Brisée
(page 236)

Unbleached all-purpose
flour, for dusting

¼ cup sugar

2 tablespoons
unsalted butter

Pinch of kosher salt

2 tablespoons
Calvados

1½ cups Martha's Pink
Applesauce (page 242)

2 small red-skinned
apples (about 12 ounces),
such as McIntosh
or Empire

3 tablespoons
red currant, sour cherry,
or raspberry jelly

1. Preheat oven to 375°F. Roll out dough to ⅛-inch thickness on a lightly floured surface. Fit into a 10-inch tart pan with a removable bottom. Trim edge of dough flush with top of pan. With a fork, pierce bottom of dough all over. Freeze 15 minutes. Line crust with parchment and fill with dried beans or pie weights.

2. Bake until edges are set and golden, about 25 minutes. Carefully remove parchment and beans. Bake until bottom is dry and golden, about 10 minutes more. Transfer to a wire rack to cool completely. Increase oven temperature to 400°F.

3. In a small saucepan, combine sugar, butter, and salt. Cook over medium-high heat, stirring until sugar dissolves, about 3 minutes. Slowly add 1 tablespoon Calvados (watch out for splatters) and simmer 30 seconds. Stir in applesauce.

4. Spread applesauce mixture evenly in cooled tart shell. Core apples, then use a mandoline or very sharp knife to slice them crosswise into almost paper-thin rings. Arrange apples over applesauce mixture, overlapping slices in concentric circles from the center out, to completely cover tart. Bake until apples are crisp-tender, about 15 minutes.

5. In a small saucepan, combine jelly and remaining 1 tablespoon Calvados. Simmer over medium heat, stirring occasionally, until slightly thickened, about 3 minutes. Brush glaze over apples. Transfer tart in pan to a wire rack to cool completely. Unmold and serve.

PEAR SKILLET CAKE

*Juicy and fragrant, Bosc pears keep their shape beautifully when cooked.
Sliced thin and fanned out over the batter, they create a whimsical flower design.
Use the 8-inch skillet called for here; in a smaller pan, the batter will bake
over the pears—though no doubt the cake will be just as delicious.* **SERVES 6 TO 8**

¾ cup plus
2 tablespoons sugar

½ vanilla bean,
split and seeds scraped

4 tablespoons unsalted
butter, room temperature,
plus more for skillet

1 cup unbleached
all-purpose flour,
plus more for skillet

½ teaspoon
baking powder

¼ teaspoon baking soda

½ teaspoon kosher salt

1 large egg

½ cup buttermilk

1 Bosc or Anjou pear,
peeled, cored, and
thinly sliced

1. Preheat oven to 375°F. In a small bowl, combine 2 tablespoons
sugar and vanilla seeds.

2. Butter an 8-inch ovenproof skillet (preferably cast-iron) and
dust with flour. In a medium bowl, whisk together flour, baking
powder, baking soda, and salt. With an electric mixer on medium
speed, beat butter and remaining ¾ cup sugar in a large bowl
until pale and fluffy, 3 to 5 minutes. Beat in egg. Add flour mixture
in three batches, alternating with buttermilk and beginning and
ending with flour; beat until combined.

3. Transfer batter to prepared skillet, smoothing top with a small
offset spatula. Arrange pears on top, fanning slices. Sprinkle with
vanilla sugar.

4. Bake until golden brown and a cake tester comes out clean,
35 to 40 minutes. Transfer to a wire rack to cool slightly before
serving.

APPLE-BOURBON POTPIES

Individual apple pies topped with golden, flaky crust are the perfect finale for a cozy fall dinner. Store-bought puff pastry (all butter, please!) makes them easy; a boozy apple filling (we used bourbon, but another whiskey or even rum works, too) makes them totally decadent. Serve warm with vanilla ice cream. **MAKES 6**

4 pounds apples
(12 to 13 medium),
preferably a combination
of Granny Smith and
Rome, peeled, cored,
and cut into 8 wedges

1 cup sugar

2 tablespoons
fresh lemon juice

¾ teaspoon kosher salt

½ teaspoon
ground allspice

6 tablespoons
unsalted butter

⅓ cup bourbon

2 tablespoons unbleached
all-purpose flour, plus
more for dusting

1 package (14 ounces)
all-butter puff pastry,
such as Dufour,
thawed if frozen

1 large egg, lightly
beaten, for egg wash

Vanilla ice cream,
for serving

1. Preheat oven to 375°F. In a large bowl, toss together apples, sugar, lemon juice, salt, and allspice. In a large straight-sided skillet, melt 3 tablespoons butter over high heat. Add half of fruit mixture and cook, stirring, 5 minutes. Reduce heat to medium-high and cook until fruit is softened, about 5 minutes more. Transfer to a bowl. Repeat with remaining 3 tablespoons butter and remaining fruit mixture. Return first batch of fruit mixture to pan. Slowly stir in bourbon (watch out for splatters). Add flour and cook, stirring, until fruit mixture thickens, about 1 minute.

2. Divide fruit mixture among six 8-ounce round baking dishes (each 5 inches in diameter). Place on a rimmed baking sheet to let cool completely.

3. On a lightly floured surface, roll out puff pastry to an 8-by-12-inch rectangle, about ⅛ inch thick. Cut out six 4-inch squares and loosely place one over filling in each dish. Cut a vent in each top. Brush pastry with egg wash. Bake until fillings are bubbling and crusts are golden, 25 to 30 minutes. Let cool about 10 minutes before serving with ice cream.

TIP:
The apple filling can
be made a day ahead
and stored in the
refrigerator; bring to
room temperature
before using.

RED-GRAPE CAKE WITH WHIPPED CRÈME FRAÎCHE

In Italy, a simple olive oil cake studded with grapes is a way to welcome the harvest. In a twist on this tradition, we've enriched it with butter and sour cream, rather than oil, for an absolutely sublime fall treat. **SERVES 8 TO 10**

6 tablespoons unsalted butter, room temperature, plus more for pan

1¼ cups unbleached all-purpose flour

1¼ teaspoons baking powder

½ teaspoon kosher salt

¾ cup granulated sugar

2 large eggs, room temperature

¼ cup sour cream, room temperature

1 teaspoon finely grated lemon zest

1¼ cups red seedless grapes, plus more for serving

¾ cup cold heavy cream

3 tablespoons confectioners' sugar

⅓ cup cold crème fraîche

1. Preheat oven to 350°F. Butter a 9-inch round cake pan and line bottom with parchment; butter parchment. In a medium bowl, whisk together flour, baking powder, and salt.

2. In a large bowl, beat together butter and granulated sugar with an electric mixer on medium-high speed until light and fluffy, about 2 minutes. Add eggs, one at a time, beating well after each addition. Fold in half of flour mixture, then sour cream and lemon zest. Stir in remaining flour mixture just to combine. Spread batter evenly in prepared pan, smoothing top with a small offset spatula. Scatter grapes over top.

3. Bake until cake pulls away from sides of pan and a cake tester comes out clean, 45 to 50 minutes. Transfer to a wire rack to cool 20 minutes. Turn out cake onto rack, remove parchment, invert cake, and cool completely.

4. In a large bowl and with an electric mixer on medium-high, whip cream and confectioners' sugar to soft peaks, about 3 minutes. Add crème fraîche and whip to firm peaks, about 2 minutes more. Serve cake with whipped crème fraîche and additional grapes.

APPLE TART WITH QUINCE

Pâte sucrée, Martha's favorite sweet piecrust, is the foundation of this artful tart: It is flaky and buttery and can be made ahead. The glossy finish on the fruit, a mix of several apples, comes from apple brandy and tangy quince paste, called membrillo *in Spain; look for it in specialty stores.* **SERVES 8**

FOR THE PÂTE SUCRÉE

2½ cups unbleached all-purpose flour, plus more for dusting

3 tablespoons granulated sugar

1 teaspoon kosher salt

2 sticks (1 cup) cold unsalted butter, cut into pieces

2 to 4 tablespoons ice-cold water

2 large egg yolks, lightly beaten

FOR THE APPLESAUCE FILLING

4 pounds McIntosh apples (12 to 13), halved, cored, and cut into 8 wedges

2 pounds other red apples (6 to 7), such as Rome, Empire, or Cortland, quartered and cored, plus 1 pound whole apples (3 to 4)

½ cup fresh lemon juice (from 3 lemons), plus more for brushing

1 large egg, lightly beaten, for egg wash

Fine sanding sugar, for sprinkling

FOR THE GLAZE

½ cup granulated sugar

3 tablespoons apple brandy, such as Calvados

3 tablespoons quince paste

¼ teaspoon kosher salt

1 tablespoon unsalted butter, room temperature

1. Make the pâte sucrée: Pulse flour, granulated sugar, and salt in a food processor until combined. Add butter and pulse just until mixture resembles coarse meal, with a few pea-size pieces of butter remaining, about 10 seconds. Drizzle in 2 tablespoons ice water, then slowly add egg yolks, pulsing until dough just holds together, about 30 seconds. Test dough at this point by squeezing a small amount together. If it is too dry, drizzle in up to 2 tablespoons more ice water, a tablespoon at a time. Turn out dough onto a piece of plastic wrap, shape into a rectangle, and wrap tightly. Refrigerate until firm, at least 1 hour or up to 2 days. (Dough can be frozen up to 3 months; thaw in refrigerator before using.)

2. On a lightly floured piece of parchment, roll out dough to a 14-by-17-inch rectangle. Using a paring knife, lightly trace a 1-inch border around perimeter of dough (this border will be folded up over the filling to form the tart crust. Transfer dough on parchment to a rimmed baking sheet and refrigerate at least 1 hour.

(continued)

TIP:
When prepping the apples for the filling, begin by cutting them in half and then coring them. Using a sharp paring knife, thinly slice crosswise, keeping the sliced halves together in sections. This will make it easy to shingle the graphic design.

3. Make the applesauce filling: In a large pot, combine McIntosh apples, 2 pounds quartered red apples, the lemon juice, and 1½ cups water. Cover and bring to a boil over high heat, stirring occasionally. Reduce heat to medium, partially cover, and cook, stirring occasionally, until apples are completely soft, about 40 minutes. To remove skins, pass apples through a medium-mesh sieve or a food mill fitted with the fine disk. (Applesauce can be stored in refrigerator up to 1 week or in freezer up to 3 months.)

4. Preheat oven to 375°F. Spread 2 cups applesauce evenly over chilled dough, leaving a 1-inch border (reserve remaining apple-sauce for another use).

5. Halve, core, and thinly slice crosswise remaining 1 pound red apples with a very sharp knife or a mandoline, reserving scraps for glaze. Shingle 6 slices into a 3-inch square on top of filling in one corner of tart. Brush with lemon juice to prevent apples from browning. Repeat process with remaining apple slices, placing them as closely as possible to the previous 3-inch square of apples and alternating the direction of the shingling in a grid pattern (you should have 4 rows of 5).

6. Fold edges of dough up and over filling to create the crust. Brush outer edges with egg wash and sprinkle generously with sanding sugar. Bake, rotating halfway through, until crust is deep golden brown all over, 45 to 55 minutes. Transfer sheet to a wire rack to cool completely.

7. Make the glaze: In a medium saucepan, cook reserved apple scraps, ½ cup water, granulated sugar, apple brandy, quince paste, and salt over low heat until scraps are very soft, about 20 minutes. Whisk in butter until melted, then strain mixture through a fine-mesh sieve, pressing on solids. Brush apples on cooled tart with glaze to coat; let dry. Serve tart at room temperature.

RASPBERRY AND PECAN BUCKLE

A buckle is another one of those beloved desserts your grandmother probably made. You'd be forgiven for calling this a coffee cake—the big difference is the generous amount of fruit in the batter, which often creates charming dents and dimples (or buckles)—as it bakes. This one makes the most of fall raspberries, before they're gone. **SERVES 12**

FOR THE TOPPING

2 cups unbleached all-purpose flour

1¼ cup packed light-brown sugar

2 teaspoons ground cinnamon

¼ teaspoon ground cardamom

½ teaspoon kosher salt

2 sticks (1 cup) cold unsalted butter, cut into small pieces

1 cup pecans, toasted (page 246) and chopped

FOR THE CAKE

1 stick (½ cup) unsalted butter, room temperature, plus more for pan

2 cups unbleached all-purpose flour

1¼ teaspoons baking powder

½ teaspoon baking soda

½ teaspoon kosher salt

1 cup granulated sugar

2 large eggs

1 cup sour cream

2 teaspoons vanilla extract

3 cups raspberries

1. Make the topping: In a medium bowl, whisk together flour, brown sugar, cinnamon, cardamom, and salt. Cut in butter using a pastry blender, or rub in with your fingers, until small clumps form. Mix in pecans. Refrigerate until ready to use.

2. Make the cake: Preheat oven to 350°F. Butter a 9-by-13-inch baking pan. Line with parchment with overhang on two long sides; butter parchment. In a medium bowl, whisk flour, baking powder, baking soda, and salt.

3. With an electric mixer on medium-high speed, beat butter and granulated sugar until pale and fluffy, about 3 minutes. Add eggs, one at a time, beating thoroughly after each and scraping down sides of bowl. Add flour mixture, sour cream, and vanilla and beat until just combined. Gently fold 2 cups raspberries into batter. Transfer batter to prepared pan and smooth top with a small offset spatula.

4. Evenly sprinkle crumb topping over batter in two batches, alternating with remaining 1 cup raspberries. Bake until a cake tester inserted into center comes out clean, about 1 hour 15 minutes. Transfer to a wire rack to cool. Serve slightly warm or at room temperature.

APPLE PIE WITH PATCHWORK CRUST

Two simple ingredients can elevate a good apple pie to something truly extraordinary: brown butter and vanilla seeds, straight from the bean. The butter, heated until it's a deep golden brown, gives the filling a rich, nutty flavor, and the vanilla adds a warm sweetness and incredible fragrance. **SERVES 8**

FOR THE CRUST

2 cups unbleached all-purpose flour, plus more for dusting

¾ teaspoon kosher salt

2 sticks (1 cup) cold unsalted butter, cut into pieces

1 large egg

2 to 4 tablespoons ice-cold water

1 tablespoon distilled white vinegar

FOR THE FILLING

4 tablespoons unsalted butter

3 pounds Granny Smith apples (6 to 7 medium), peeled, cored, and cut into eighths

1 tablespoon lemon juice

¼ cup unbleached all-purpose flour

½ teaspoon kosher salt

¾ cup granulated sugar

½ cup light-brown sugar

1 vanilla bean, split and seeds scraped

1 large egg, lightly beaten, for egg wash

Coarse sanding sugar, for sprinkling

1. Make the crust: Pulse flour and salt in a food processor until combined. Add butter and process just until mixture resembles coarse meal, with a few pea-size pieces remaining, about 10 seconds. In a small bowl, beat together egg, 2 tablespoons ice water, and vinegar. Add to flour mixture and pulse just until incorporated, about ten times more. If dough is too dry, add up to 2 tablespoons more ice water, a tablespoon at a time. Divide dough in half, pat one into a disk and the other into a rectangle, and wrap in plastic. Refrigerate until firm, at least 1 hour or up to 2 days.

2. Make the filling: In a small saucepan, melt butter over medium-low heat and cook, swirling pan occasionally, until butter is golden brown and fragrant, about 8 minutes; let cool. In a large bowl, toss together apples and lemon juice. In another large bowl, combine flour, salt, granulated and brown sugars, and vanilla seeds. Add browned butter to apples. Stir in flour mixture.

3. Roll out disk of dough to just under ¼-inch thickness on a lightly floured surface and fit into a 9-inch glass pie dish. Place apples in piecrust. Transfer to refrigerator to chill while making top crust. Roll out rectangle to ¼-inch thick. Using a pastry wheel or sharp knife, cut dough into 21 two-inch squares. Transfer to a parchment-lined baking sheet and chill until firm, about 10 minutes. Lay a row of 3 squares across either end of pie, overlapping slightly; continue with 2 rows of 5 squares, finishing with a center row of 5.

4. Preheat oven to 425°F with a rack in lowest position and a foil-lined baking sheet below to catch drips. Brush pie with egg wash and sprinkle with sanding sugar. Bake 15 minutes. Reduce temperature to 375°F and bake until browned, about 1 hour. Tent pie with foil and continue to bake until bubbling, about 20 minutes more. Transfer to a wire rack to cool, at least 6 hours, before serving.

TIP:

For this double-crust dough, white
vinegar is added for insurance.
You won't taste it, but it helps inhibit the
formation of gluten, making it easier
to achieve a flaky, tender crust
and for patterns to hold their shapes.
You could also use apple-cider
vinegar or even vodka.

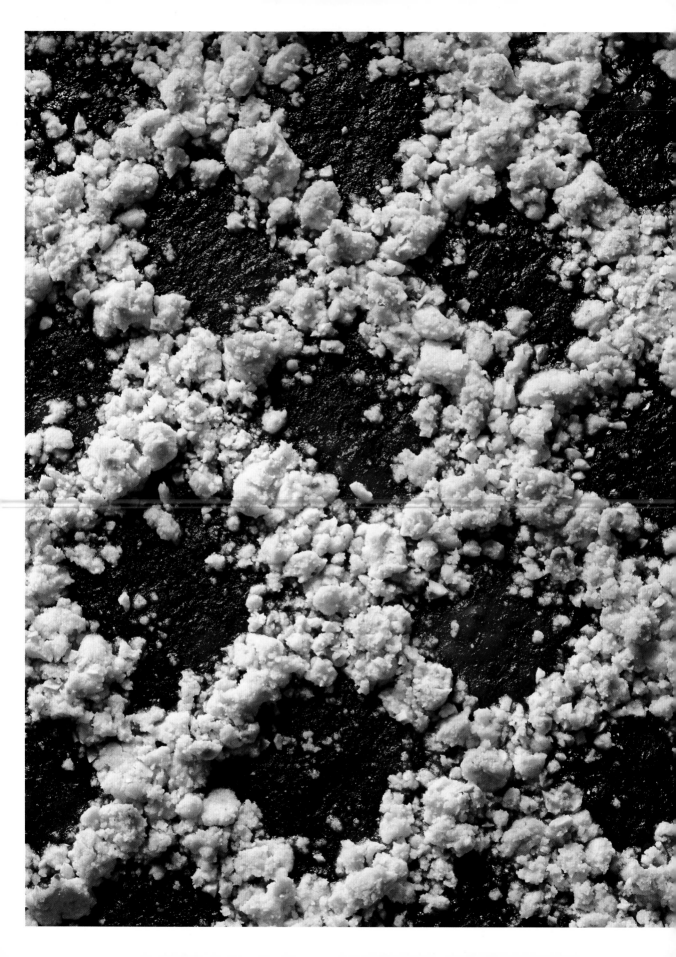

LINZER CRUMBLE PIE WITH CRANBERRY-RASPBERRY JAM

An easy twist on the classic Austrian Linzer torte, this slab pie is made with a buttery press-in hazelnut shortbread crust and a brightly flavored cranberry-and-raspberry jam filling. Instead of rolling pastry strips for a complicated lattice topping, you can mimic the look by adding more shortbread in a loose crisscross crumble. **SERVES 12**

FOR THE FILLING

1¼ pounds fresh
or frozen cranberries

12 ounces raspberries

2¾ cups sugar

1 vanilla bean,
split and seeds scraped,
pod reserved

FOR THE CRUST

Vegetable oil
cooking spray

3 sticks (1½ cups) plus
1 tablespoon unsalted
butter, room temperature

2 cups sugar

4 cups unbleached
all-purpose flour

2½ teaspoons kosher salt

1½ cups skinned
hazelnuts, toasted
(page 246) and
finely chopped

1. Make the filling: In a large saucepan, bring cranberries, raspberries, sugar, and vanilla seeds and pod to a boil, stirring occasionally. Continue cooking, stirring occasionally, until fruit is soft, about 10 minutes total. Pass through a fine-mesh sieve, pressing on solids to extract liquid; discard solids (you should have 3 cups liquid). Let cool completely. Filling can be stored in the refrigerator for up to 1 week.

2. Make the crust: Preheat oven to 350°F. Coat a 12-by-17-inch rimmed baking sheet with cooking spray. Line with parchment, leaving overhang on long sides. Spray parchment.

3. With an electric mixer on medium-high speed, beat 3 sticks butter with sugar in a large bowl until light and fluffy, about 3 minutes. Reduce speed to low, add flour and salt, and beat until dough forms clumps but does not completely hold together. Mix in hazelnuts until just combined. Reserve 1½ cups dough; press remaining dough into prepared baking sheet in an even layer. Using your fingertips, rub remaining 1 tablespoon butter into reserved 1½ cups dough until larger clumps form.

4. Spread jam filling evenly over bottom crust. Crumble remaining dough on top in a lattice pattern. Bake 30 minutes. Cover with foil and continue baking until jam is bubbling, about 15 minutes more. Transfer pan to a wire rack to cool completely. Use a paring knife to release short sides of crust from pan, then use parchment to lift pie out of pan and onto a cutting board. Cut into squares or triangles to serve.

APPLE FRITTERS

The fruit-studded, doughnut-like treats come together quickly and make an addictively delicious snack on a chilly day. If you're avoiding dairy, swap almond milk for the whole milk and margarine for the butter. **MAKES 3 DOZEN**

2 cups unbleached all-purpose flour

¼ cup plus 2 tablespoons granulated sugar

2¼ teaspoons baking powder

1 teaspoon kosher salt

¾ cup whole milk

2 large eggs, room temperature

2 tablespoons unsalted butter, melted

½ teaspoon vanilla extract

2 sweet apples, such as Rome, McIntosh, or Gala, peeled, cored, and cut into ¼-inch pieces (about 3 cups)

Safflower oil or other neutral oil, for frying

Confectioners' sugar, for dusting

1. In a large bowl, whisk together flour, granulated sugar, baking powder, and salt. In another bowl, whisk together milk, eggs, butter, and vanilla. Gently fold milk mixture into flour mixture until just combined. Fold in apples.

2. Heat 2 inches of oil in a medium heavy-bottomed pot over medium-high heat until an instant-read thermometer registers 350°F. Set a wire rack in a rimmed baking sheet.

3. Working in batches, drop heaping tablespoons of dough into oil. (A small ice-cream scoop works especially well for creating uniform-size fritters.) Cook, turning once, until puffed and golden, 3 to 4 minutes. Transfer to rack with a slotted spoon. Let cool slightly, dust with confectioners' sugar, and serve.

PEAR AND CRANBERRY PIE

Pears and cranberries make a perfect pair, especially when poached in spiced wine. Poaching fruit requires some advance prep: The longer the soak, the more luscious the fruit will be (for how-tos, see page 244). To embellish the dessert, cut shapes from the pâte brisée crust with a one-inch cookie cutter, like the flower petal one used here. **SERVES 8**

1 bottle (750 milliliters) dry white wine, such as Sauvignon Blanc

1 cup granulated sugar

2 cinnamon sticks

1 star anise pod

1 vanilla bean, split and seeds scraped

2 cups fresh or frozen cranberries

4 or 5 firm but ripe Bosc pears, peeled, quartered, and cored

Unbleached all-purpose flour, for dusting

2 disks Pâte Brisée (page 236)

1 egg, lightly beaten, for egg wash

Fine sanding sugar, for sprinkling

1. In a wide saucepan, bring wine, granulated sugar, cinnamon, star anise, vanilla seeds, and cranberries to a boil, stirring occasionally. Reduce to a simmer, add pears, and cover with a round of parchment, pressing it directly on surface of pears. Cook until pears are tender when pierced with a paring knife, 20 to 30 minutes. Using a slotted spoon, transfer fruit to a heatproof bowl. Bring liquid to a boil, and cook until thick, syrupy, and reduced to 2 cups. Discard cinnamon and star anise. Pour liquid over pears; refrigerate until cool, at least 30 minutes or up to overnight.

2. On a lightly floured surface, roll out a disk of dough to a 13-inch round. Gently fit into bottom and up sides of a 9-inch pie plate (do not stretch dough). Transfer to refrigerator to chill.

3. Preheat oven to 375°F with a rack in center and a foil-lined baking sheet on a rack below to catch any drips. On a lightly floured surface, roll out remaining disk of dough to a 13-inch round. Transfer to a parchment-lined unrimmed baking sheet. Using a 1-inch cookie cutter, cut out a decorative pattern over surface, reserving cutouts to decorate. Freeze until firm, 15 minutes.

4. Using a slotted spoon, remove pears and cranberries from poaching liquid and blot dry with paper towels. Arrange pears in prepared pie dish, then add cranberries. Brush overhang with egg wash. Place top crust over filling; press edges to seal with bottom crust. Using kitchen shears, trim dough to a ½-inch overhang. Tuck overhang under so edges are flush with rim. Brush edges with egg wash and decorate with cutouts. Brush entire surface with egg wash and sprinkle with sanding sugar. Bake 20 minutes, then reduce oven temperature to 375°F and continue baking until crust is evenly browned (if browning too quickly, tent edges with foil), 45 to 60 minutes. Transfer to a wire rack to cool completely.

APPLE AND BLACKBERRY CAKE

This beauty captures the transition from summer to fall in one delicious dish: a tender cake that brings the last of the garden's fat blackberries together with early-season apples. Serve each slice with a generous dollop of whipped cream, or present it plain—this cake is stunning just as it is. **SERVES 12**

6 tablespoons unsalted butter, melted, plus 2 tablespoons, cut into pieces, plus more for pan

Granulated sugar, for pan

1½ cups unbleached all-purpose flour

2 teaspoons baking powder

½ teaspoon kosher salt

¾ cup plus 2 tablespoons packed light-brown sugar

½ cup whole milk

2 large eggs, room temperature

4 Honeycrisp or McIntosh apples (about 1½ pounds), peeled, cored, and cut into 8 wedges

1 cup blackberries (about 5 ounces)

¼ teaspoon ground cinnamon

Whipped Cream (page 246), for serving (optional)

1. Preheat oven to 375°F. Butter a 9-inch springform pan and dust with granulated sugar. In a medium bowl, whisk together flour, baking powder, and salt. In another medium bowl, whisk together melted butter, ¾ cup brown sugar, the milk, and eggs. Whisk egg mixture into flour mixture until combined.

2. Spread batter evenly into prepared pan. Arrange apple wedges over batter and sprinkle with blackberries. Gently press fruit into batter. Combine remaining 2 tablespoons brown sugar and the cinnamon in a small bowl, and sprinkle over fruit. Dot with remaining 2 tablespoons butter. Bake until top is dark gold, apples are tender, and a cake tester comes out clean, about 55 minutes. Transfer to a wire rack to cool completely before removing outer ring from pan. Serve with whipped cream, if desired.

TIP:
Keep a dry pastry
brush handy
to remove
any excess flour
while rolling
out the dough.

FIG AND ALMOND CROSTATA

Similar to a French galette, an Italian crostata has a free-form, rustic charm, with its dough folded up around the filling. You can make this basic piecrust up to two days before and pick up piles of plump, fresh figs at the market the morning of. The fruit gets even sweeter as it cooks, perfectly complementing the salty almond filling and buttery crust. **SERVES 8**

FOR THE CRUST

1¼ cups unbleached all-purpose flour, plus more for dusting

½ teaspoon kosher salt

½ teaspoon sugar

1 stick (½ cup) cold unsalted butter, cut into pieces

2 to 4 tablespoons ice-cold water

1 large egg, lightly beaten, for egg wash

FOR THE FILLING

½ cup blanched almonds

½ cup sugar

1 large egg

4 tablespoons unsalted butter

2 teaspoons unbleached all-purpose flour

¼ teaspoon vanilla extract

Pinch of kosher salt

1 pound ripe fresh figs (about 16), stemmed and thinly sliced crosswise

1 tablespoon fresh lemon juice

1. Make the crust: Pulse flour, salt, and sugar in a food processor until combined. Add butter and pulse until mixture resembles coarse meal, with a few pea-size pieces of butter remaining. Drizzle with 2 tablespoons ice water. Pulse until dough is crumbly but holds together when squeezed, with a few pea-size pieces remaining. If dough is too dry, add up to 2 tablespoons more ice water, 1 tablespoon at a time, and pulse. Don't overmix. Turn dough out onto a large piece of plastic wrap. Fold plastic over dough; shape into a 1-inch-thick disk. Wrap tightly and refrigerate until firm, at least 1 hour or up to 3 days.

2. Make the filling: Pulse almonds and sugar in a food processor until finely ground. Add egg, butter, flour, vanilla, and salt and pulse until smooth. In a medium bowl, combine figs and lemon juice.

3. Preheat oven to 350°F. On a floured piece of parchment paper, roll out dough to a 14-inch round with a floured rolling pin. Spread almond filling in center, leaving a 2-inch border; then top with fig mixture. Fold border over edge of filling, pleating all around; press down gently to seal. In a small bowl, mix beaten egg with 1 teaspoon water. Brush crust with egg wash, brushing under folds to help seal.

4. Transfer crostata on parchment to a rimmed baking sheet. Bake until crust is golden brown, about 1 hour. Transfer baking sheet to a wire rack to cool at least 30 minutes. To serve, cut crostata into wedges.

PEAR-AND-FRANGIPANE PASTRIES

Your guests will think they fainted and awoke in a Parisian patisserie when they taste one of these delicate pastry rounds, topped with tender poached pears and the velvety almond custard known as frangipane. Plan ahead for this refined dessert, as the steps, including multiple rises and chilling, take time. The dough can be made and frozen up to two weeks ahead, and pears can (and really should) be poached at least the day before. **MAKES 16**

FOR THE DOUGH

1 envelope (¼ ounce or 2¼ teaspoons) active dry yeast (not rapid-rise)

1 cup warm milk (110°F)

1 vanilla bean, split and seeds scraped

4½ cups plus 2 tablespoons unbleached all-purpose flour (1¼ pounds), plus more for dusting

½ cup sugar

1 tablespoon kosher salt

4 sticks (2 cups) unsalted butter, room temperature, cut into tablespoons

2 large whole eggs plus 1 large egg yolk

FOR THE POACHED PEARS

1 bottle (750 milliliters) dry white wine, such as Sauvignon Blanc

Grated zest of 1 lemon plus 2 tablespoons fresh lemon juice

1 cup sugar

2 cinnamon sticks

1 vanilla bean, split and seeds scraped

8 small pears, such as Bartlett (about 2 pounds), stems left on, peeled, halved lengthwise, and cored

FOR THE FRANGIPANE

4 tablespoons unsalted butter, room temperature

¼ cup sugar

2 large eggs, room temperature

½ cup finely ground blanched almonds

1 tablespoon dark rum

½ teaspoon pure almond extract

2 tablespoons unbleached all-purpose flour

1. Make the dough: In a small bowl, sprinkle yeast over milk; stir until dissolved. Let sit until foamy, about 5 minutes. Stir in vanilla seeds. In the bowl of a mixer fitted with the dough-hook attachment, mix together 4½ cups flour, the sugar, salt, and 4 tablespoons butter on low speed until mixture resembles coarse meal, 3 to 4 minutes. Add yeast mixture; mix until dough just comes together. Add eggs and yolk; mix until just combined, 2 to 3 minutes (do not overmix).

2. Turn out dough onto a lightly floured surface. Gently knead to form a smooth ball, about 30 seconds. Wrap dough tightly in plastic and refrigerate at least 2 hours or up to overnight.

3. In the bowl of a mixer fitted with the paddle attachment, beat together remaining 3 sticks 4 table-spoons butter and 2 tablespoons flour. Shape butter mixture into a 10-by-12-inch rectangle on a piece of plastic. Wrap and refrigerate at least 15 minutes or up to 1 day.

(Remove butter mixture from refrigerator and let stand at room temperature until it is the same consistency as the dough.)

4. On a lightly floured surface, roll out dough to a 10-by-18-inch rectangle, about ¼ inch thick, keeping corners square. (Remove any excess flour from dough with a dry pastry brush.) With a short side facing you, spread room-temperature butter mixture over two-thirds of dough. Fold unbuttered third over as you would a business letter, followed by the remaining third. (This seals in the butter.) Roll out dough again to a 10-by-18-inch rectangle, then fold into thirds as described above; wrap and refrigerate 1 hour. (This completes the first of three turns.) Repeat rolling and folding process two more times, refrigerating at least 1 hour between turns. Wrap tightly in plastic and refrigerate at least 4 hours or up to overnight. Dough can also be frozen, tightly wrapped in plastic, up to 2 weeks (thaw in refrigerator overnight before using).

5. Poach the pears: In a large saucepan, bring wine, lemon zest and juice, sugar, cinnamon, vanilla seeds, and 2 cups water to a boil. Reduce to a simmer, add pears, and cover with a parch-ment round to keep fruit submerged (for how-tos, see page 244). Cook, occasionally turning pears by gently rotating the stems with your fingertips, until pears are tender when pierced with a paring knife, about 20 minutes. With a slotted spoon, transfer pears to a heatproof bowl. Return poaching liquid to a boil and continue cooking until syrupy and reduced by half, 10 to 12 minutes. Pour syrup over pears and refrigerate, covered, at least 4 hours or preferably overnight.

6. Make the frangipane: In the bowl of a mixer fitted with the paddle attachment or a mini food processor, beat together butter and sugar until light and fluffy, about 3 minutes. Add 1 egg, almonds, rum, almond extract, and flour and beat until smooth.

7. Using a slotted spoon, remove pears from poaching liquid and pat dry with paper towels. On a lightly floured surface, roll out dough to a 12-by-20-inch rectangle about ¼ inch thick. Using a 3½-inch round cutter, cut out 16 rounds and divide between 2 parchment-lined baking sheets. Fill each pear half with about 2 tea-spoons frangipane and place cut-side down in centers rounds. Cover with plastic wrap and let stand in a warm place until doubled in bulk, about 45 minutes.

8. Preheat oven to 375°F. In a small bowl, lightly beat remaining egg. Brush rounds of dough with egg wash, avoiding pears. Bake, rotating half-way through, until pastries are evenly browned, 20 to 25 minutes. Transfer to a wire rack to cool completely. Serve at room temperature.

TIP:
The rolling and folding process needs to be repeated three times, chilling the dough at least an hour between each. To help you remember how many turns have been completed, mark the dough after each one: make one mark for the first turn, two for the second, and three for the third.

APPLE WEAVE PIE

Create this strudel-like stunner by weaving strips of puff pastry over cognac-tossed apples in a braid-like fashion. It's worth seeking out all-butter puff pastry, and, for best results, thaw it in the refrigerator the night before using. **SERVES 10**

FOR THE FILLING

5 apples (about 1½ pounds), such as Empire, Rome, or Cortland, peeled, halved, cored, and cut into 8 wedges

¾ cup granulated sugar

1 vanilla bean, split and seeds scraped

3 tablespoons cognac

1 teaspoon finely grated lemon zest plus 2 tablespoons fresh juice

¼ teaspoon kosher salt

2 teaspoons unbleached all-purpose flour

2 tablespoons unsalted butter, cut into small pieces

FOR THE PASTRY

Unbleached all-purpose flour, for dusting

1 package (14 ounces) all-butter puff pastry, such as Dufour, thawed if frozen

1 large egg, lightly beaten

Coarse sanding sugar, for sprinkling

Vanilla ice cream, for serving (optional)

1. Make the filling: Preheat oven to 350°F. In a large bowl, toss together apples, granulated sugar, vanilla seeds, cognac, lemon zest and juice, salt, and flour. Transfer to a 9-by-13-inch baking dish and dot with butter. Bake until apples are tender, about 40 minutes. Let cool completely.

2. Make the pastry: Increase oven to 400°F. On a piece of lightly floured parchment, roll out pastry to a 12½-by-16½-inch rectangle. Using tip of a paring knife, lightly score pastry into thirds lengthwise, being careful not to cut all the way through. Cut ¾-inch-wide strips crosswise along the two outer thirds, reserving center third for filling. Transfer the pastry on parchment to a baking sheet (if pastry becomes too soft, freeze until firm).

3. Arrange filling evenly in center third of pastry. Freeze 20 minutes. Whisk egg with 1 teaspoon water; lightly brush strips with egg wash. Alternating from one side to the other, fold strips evenly over filling in an overlapping braiding pattern.

4. Lightly brush top with egg wash and generously sprinkle with sanding sugar. Bake 20 minutes, then reduce oven temperature to 350°F and bake 20 minutes more. Let cool to room temperature. Slice and serve with vanilla ice cream, if desired.

Concord Grape–Lavender
Sorbet

Cranberry-Port
Sorbet

Pear–Red Wine
Sorbet

SORBETS

Sorbet calls for a simple juice-to-sugar ratio that you can customize to your desire. In this trio, the crimson-hued cranberry version is tart, sweet, and spiked with port, which helps preserve the pleasing texture of the frozen treat. Concord grapes bring their trademark flavor and deep purple hue to this sorbet, while organic fresh lavender adds a delicate, floral note. Pear and red wine join to create a cooling pretty-in-pink dessert. **SERVES 12**

CRANBERRY-PORT SORBET

12 ounces fresh or thawed frozen cranberries
(about 3½ cups)

1½ cups sugar

1 cup ruby port

3 strips lemon zest
(each about 3 inches long)
plus 1 tablespoon fresh lemon juice

1. In a medium saucepan, bring cranberries, sugar, port, lemon zest, lemon juice, and 3 cups water to a boil. Reduce heat to medium-low. Simmer, stirring occasionally, until cranberries are tender, about 20 minutes. Let cool for 15 minutes. Remove zest. Transfer to a shallow baking dish. Freeze until solid, at least 6 hours or up to a day.

2. With a fork, break frozen mixture into large pieces. In two batches, purée in a food processor until completely smooth, 2 to 3 minutes per batch. Transfer to an airtight container and freeze until ready to serve (sorbet will be soft).

CONCORD GRAPE–LAVENDER SORBET

½ cup sugar

2 tablespoons fresh organic lavender flowers

1 pound Concord grapes, stems removed

1. In a small saucepan, bring sugar and ½ cup water to a boil, stirring until sugar dissolves. Remove from heat and add lavender. Let steep 10 minutes. Strain through a fine-mesh sieve set over a medium bowl, pressing on solids; discard solids. Refrigerate syrup until cold, about 15 minutes.

2. In a blender, purée grapes until smooth. Strain through a fine-mesh sieve set over a medium bowl, pressing on solids; discard solids. Stir in lavender syrup, cover tightly with plastic, and refrigerate until cold, at least 1 hour or up to 2 hours.

3. Freeze and churn mixture in an ice cream maker according to manufacturer's instructions. Transfer to an airtight container. Freeze for at least 1 hour before serving.

PEAR–RED WINE SORBET

1 cup dry red wine

¾ cup sugar

1 pound ripe Bartlett pears,
peeled, cored, and cut into
1-inch pieces (2 cups)

2 tablespoons fresh lemon juice

Pinch of kosher salt

1. In a small saucepan, bring wine, 1¼ cups water, and sugar to a boil over medium heat, stirring often, until sugar dissolves. Add pears, reduce heat, and simmer until tender, 5 to 10 minutes. Stir in lemon juice and salt; cool completely. Transfer to a shallow baking dish. Freeze until solid, at least 6 hours or up to a day.

2. With a fork, break frozen mixture into large pieces. In two batches, purée in a food processor until completely smooth, 2 to 3 minutes per batch. Transfer to an airtight container and freeze until ready to serve (sorbet will be soft).

APPLE CROSTATA WITH CHEDDAR CRUST

In this casual yet elegant tart, cheddar cheese gets baked right into the crust, making an ideal pairing with sweet apples. The pie dough makes enough for two 11-inch crostatas, so you can freeze one disk, up to one month, or double the fruit filling. **SERVES 8 TO 10**

FOR THE CRUST

2 1/2 cups unbleached all-purpose flour, plus more for dusting

1 teaspoon kosher salt

2 sticks (1 cup) cold unsalted butter, cut into small pieces

1/4 to 1/2 cup ice water

1 cup shredded sharp white cheddar cheese

1 large egg, lightly beaten, for egg wash

Coarse sanding sugar, for sprinkling

FOR THE FILLING

2 tart apples, such as Granny Smith or Pink Lady, peeled, cored, and sliced into 1/2-inch wedges

2 McIntosh apples, peeled, cored, and sliced into 1/2-inch wedges

1/2 cup granulated sugar

2 tablespoons unbleached all-purpose flour

2 tablespoons fresh lemon juice

1/4 teaspoon ground cinnamon

1/4 cup apricot preserves

1. Make the crust: Pulse flour and salt in a food processor until combined. Add butter and pulse until mixture resembles coarse meal, with a few pea-size pieces of butter remaining, about 10 seconds. Drizzle 1/4 cup ice water evenly over mixture. Pulse until dough just holds together. If it is too dry, add up to 1/4 cup water, 1 tablespoon at a time, and pulse. Don't overmix. Add cheese; pulse until combined. Divide dough in half, pat each half into a disk, and wrap in plastic. Refrigerate until firm, about 30 minutes or up to overnight. (Dough can be frozen up to 1 month; thaw before using.)

2. Roll out dough to a 13-inch round, about 1/8 inch thick, on a lightly floured surface. Transfer to a parchment-lined baking sheet. Refrigerate for 20 minutes.

3. Make the filling: In a large bowl, toss together apples, granulated sugar, flour, lemon juice, and cinnamon.

4. Spread filling over dough, leaving a 1 1/2-inch border. Fold border over edge of filling, brush with egg wash, and sprinkle with sanding sugar. Refrigerate until edges are firm, about 30 minutes. Meanwhile, preheat oven to 375°F.

5. Bake crostata until apples are tender and crust is golden, about 1 hour 20 minutes. Let cool slightly. Meanwhile, in a small saucepan, heat apricot preserves. Strain through a fine-mesh sieve, pressing on solids; discard solids. Brush apples with apricot preserves and serve.

QUINCE PIE

Under the buttery puff pastry crust is a beautiful rosy filling of quince, gently poached in warm spices and dessert wine. If you haven't discovered the magic of quince, give it a try. The awkward-looking cousin to pears and apples shows up in farmers' markets each fall. It has a woody texture and sharp taste when raw, but cooking turns it tender, fragrant, and the prettiest pink. **SERVES 8**

FOR THE FILLING

3 cups sweet dessert wine, such as Sauternes

½ cup granulated sugar

4 tablespoons unsalted butter

4 quinces, peeled, cored, and quartered

4 green cardamom pods, crushed

2 cinnamon sticks

1 piece (2 inches) peeled fresh ginger, thinly sliced

1 vanilla bean, split and seeds scraped, pod reserved

FOR THE CRUST

1 package (14 ounces) all-butter puff pastry, such as Dufour, thawed if frozen

Unbleached all-purpose flour, for dusting

1 large egg, lightly beaten, for egg wash

Coarse sanding sugar, for sprinkling

1. Make the filling: In a large pot, bring 2 cups water, the wine, granulated sugar, butter, quinces, cardamom, cinnamon sticks, ginger, and vanilla seeds and pod to a simmer over medium heat. Cover with a round of parchment, pressing it directly onto surface of quinces (for how-tos, see page 244). Cook until quinces are soft and rosy pink, about 2 hours. Discard ginger and vanilla and cardamom pods.

2. Make the crust: Preheat oven to 400°F. Roll out puff pastry to a 12-by-15-inch rectangle on a lightly floured piece of parchment; transfer pastry on parchment to a baking sheet. Freeze until firm, about 30 minutes.

3. Cut dough in half lengthwise to form two 6-by-15-inch rectangles. Using a slotted spoon, transfer quince onto a puff pastry rectangle, leaving a 1-inch border. (There will be a small pool of liquid.) Brush border with egg wash. Top with remaining puff pastry, pressing edges to seal. Brush top with egg wash and sprinkle with sanding sugar. Freeze until firm, about 15 minutes.

4. Cut six 2-inch slits, spaced 2 inches apart, along pastry top for steam vents. Bake until puffed and golden, about 45 minutes. Slice pie into triangular pieces. Serve immediately.

NaNAUTUMN

CARAMEL–APPLE BREAD PUDDING

Remember biting into a caramel apple when you were a kid? The sweetness of the candy, the juicy freshness of the fruit? This decadent dessert is like that, only warmer, richer, and with just enough custard and airy, eggy brioche to hold it all together. Look for tart apples, like Pink Lady. **SERVES 8 TO 10**

FOR THE CARAMEL

1½ cups granulated sugar

6 tablespoons unsalted butter

⅓ cup heavy cream

2 teaspoons vanilla extract

1 teaspoon kosher salt

FOR THE BREAD PUDDING

Unsalted butter, for pan

1 cup heavy cream

1 cup whole milk

3 large eggs

⅓ cup packed light-brown sugar

¾ teaspoon ground cinnamon

¼ teaspoon freshly grated nutmeg

8 ounces brioche, preferably day-old, cut into 1-inch cubes (about 6 cups)

2 tart red apples, such as Pink Lady, peeled, cored, and sliced crosswise into ¼-inch-thick pieces

Vanilla ice cream, for serving

1. Make the caramel: In a medium saucepan, boil granulated sugar and ¼ cup water until sugar dissolves, about 5 minutes, stirring and brushing down sides of pan with a wet pastry brush to prevent sugar crystals from forming. Without stirring, continue to cook, swirling occasionally, until mixture is deep golden brown, about 5 minutes. Remove from heat. Whisk in butter, then heavy cream (it will bubble up), vanilla, and salt. (You should have about 1½ cups.) Let cool while preparing bread pudding.

2. Make the bread pudding: Preheat oven to 350°F with a rack in lower third and a foil-lined baking sheet on the rack below. Lightly butter a 9-inch pie dish.

3. In a large bowl, whisk together cream, milk, eggs, brown sugar, cinnamon, and nutmeg. Add brioche and gently toss to coat. Set aside at room temperature for 30 minutes to soak.

4. In another large bowl, toss apples with 1 cup caramel until coated. Gently fold apple mixture into bread mixture until just combined. Transfer mixture to prepared pie dish and pour remaining juices over top, filling just to edge of pie dish (you may not need all the juices). Cover with parchment-lined foil.

5. Bake for 45 minutes. Uncover and continue to bake until bread pudding is golden brown and set in center, 30 to 35 minutes more. Transfer to a wire rack to cool at least 10 minutes before serving topped with vanilla ice cream and remaining caramel.

PEAR AND APPLE PHYLLO CRISP

If you've been hesitant to work with delicate phyllo dough, let this sweet-crisp treat be your introduction. It's surprisingly easy to layer the papery sheets of store-bought dough with a buttery, nutty filling, creating a base for thin-sliced pears and apples. Simply defrost frozen phyllo in the refrigerator overnight, and cover with a damp towel while you work, to keep it from drying out. **SERVES 8**

⅓ cup plain fresh
bread crumbs
(from 1 slice; see Tip)

½ cup pecans,
toasted (page 246) and
finely chopped

¼ cup sugar, plus
more for sprinkling

½ teaspoon ground
cinnamon, plus more
for dusting

6 sheets frozen phyllo
dough (11½ by 15 inches
each), thawed

1 stick (½ cup) unsalted
butter, melted

3 small firm pears,
such as Seckel or Forelle

2 Granny Smith
apples, peeled

1. Preheat oven to 400°F with a rack in top position. In a small bowl, combine bread crumbs, pecans, sugar, and cinnamon.

2. Line a baking sheet with parchment and top with a phyllo sheet. Brush phyllo all over with butter and sprinkle pecan mixture evenly over top. Repeat four times. Top with remaining phyllo sheet and brush with all but 2 tablespoons butter.

3. Slice pears and apples crosswise ⅛ inch thick; save scraps for snacking and discard seeds. Arrange pear and apple slices in a single layer on phyllo, leaving space between fruit and a ¼-inch border around edges. Brush fruit with remaining 2 tablespoons butter. Sprinkle with sugar and dust with cinnamon. Bake, rotating sheet halfway through, until phyllo is golden brown and fruit is soft, 28 to 32 minutes. Let cool slightly. Cut into 8 pieces and serve.

TIP:
To make bread crumbs,
toss stale bread in
a blender or food
processor and pulse to
desired crumb size.
If you prefer fresh
bread, first dry
it out in a 300°F oven
for 15 minutes. (Store, in
a resealable bag,
in the refrigerator
for up to 1 month or in
the freezer for
up to 3 months.)

CRANBERRY SKILLET CAKE

This berry-studded cake is festive enough for the holiday table but comes together so easily, you can mix it up anytime. Pop it in the oven as you're sitting down for dinner. If you have leftovers, no one will judge you for digging in at breakfast the next day. **SERVES 8**

6 tablespoons
unsalted butter, melted,
plus more for pan

1¼ cups cranberries,
partially thawed if frozen

¾ cup plus
2 tablespoons sugar

1 cup unbleached
all-purpose flour

1¼ teaspoons
baking powder

½ teaspoon kosher salt

½ cup whole milk

1 large egg

1. Preheat oven to 350°F. Butter a 10-inch cast-iron skillet. In a medium bowl, stir together cranberries and 2 tablespoons sugar. In a large bowl, whisk together flour, baking powder, salt, and remaining ¾ cup sugar. In a small bowl, whisk together milk and egg, then whisk in butter. Whisk milk mixture into flour mixture until combined.

2. Pour batter into skillet and scatter cranberries on top. Bake until center springs back when lightly touched, 25 to 30 minutes. Let cool for 15 minutes before serving (or let sit at room temperature for up to 8 hours).

TIP:
Prep the cranberries
by first rinsing
them in a bowl of
cold water. Discard
any bruised or
shriveled berries.

PEAR-CRANBERRY SLAB PIE

This is the definition of a crowd-pleaser: all the delectable parts of a pie— the flaky crust, the sweet-tart fruit filling, the nutty, brown-sugary crumble topping—baked up in one oversized pan. Cut into squares for easy serving; they can even be picked up and eaten out of hand. **SERVES 24**

FOR THE CRUST

3¾ cups unbleached all-purpose flour, plus more for dusting

2½ teaspoons kosher salt

1½ teaspoons granulated sugar

3 sticks (1½ cups) cold unsalted butter, cut into small pieces

½ to ¾ cup ice-cold water

FOR THE CRUMBLE TOPPING

1½ cups pecan halves, toasted (page 246) and chopped

1½ cups unbleached all-purpose flour

1 cup old-fashioned rolled oats

1½ teaspoons kosher salt

2 sticks (1 cup) unsalted butter, room temperature

½ cup packed light-brown sugar

1 cup granulated sugar

FOR THE FILLING

5¼ pounds firm, ripe Bosc or Anjou pears (about 12), peeled, cored, and cut into ½-inch wedges

1 tablespoon plus 1 teaspoon fresh lemon juice

1 vanilla bean, split and seeds scraped

1 cup granulated sugar

¼ cup unbleached all-purpose flour

½ teaspoon kosher salt

1¼ teaspoons ground cinnamon

2 cups fresh or frozen cranberries

1. Make the crust: Pulse flour, salt, and granulated sugar in a food processor until combined. Add butter and pulse until mixture resembles coarse meal, with a few pea-size pieces of butter remaining. Drizzle with ½ cup ice water and pulse until incorporated. If too dry, add up to ¼ cup more, 1 tablespoon at a time. Turn out dough onto a piece of plastic wrap. Form into a flat rectangle, wrap tightly, and refrigerate at least 1 hour or up to 2 days. Roll out to a 14-by-19-inch rectangle on a lightly floured surface. Fit into a 12-by-17-inch rimmed baking sheet; fold under any overhang, tucking it into the pan. Refrigerate at least 1 hour or up to 8 hours.

2. Make the crumble topping: In a medium bowl, stir together pecans, flour, oats, and salt. With an electric mixer on medium-high speed, beat together butter and both sugars in a large bowl until pale and fluffy, about 3 minutes Add pecan mixture and beat just until combined. Work mixture with your fingers until large clumps form. Refrigerate until ready to use, up to 1 week.

3. Make the filling: Preheat oven to 400°F. In a large bowl, combine pears, lemon juice, and vanilla seeds. Stir in sugar, flour, salt, and cinnamon. Spread mixture evenly in crust and top with cranberries. Crumble large clumps of topping evenly over filling. Bake pie until crumble is golden brown and filling is bubbling, about 1 hour. Transfer to a wire rack to cool at least 1 hour before cutting into squares.

TIP:
Crisp, juicy, and
sweetly aromatic,
Golden Delicious
is a mellow
apple that holds
its shape well
in cooking.

APPLE CUSTARD PIE

This gorgeous pie delivers rich caramel, apples, and creamy custard in a nest of kataifi, *a shredded phyllo dough commonly used in Middle Eastern baked goods. To form the delicate-looking crust, look for the preshredded pastry in the freezer section of the grocery store; then simply thaw, arrange in the pan, and brush with butter.* **SERVES 8**

FOR THE CRUST

3 ounces frozen kataifi (shredded phyllo), thawed (1 packed cup)

3 tablespoons unsalted butter, melted

FOR THE CARAMELIZED APPLES

1 tablespoon unsalted butter

5 baking apples (about 2½ pounds total), such as Golden Delicious or Pink Lady, peeled, cored, and sliced into ½-inch wedges

¼ cup sugar

FOR THE CARAMEL

¾ cup sugar

1 cup heavy cream

FOR THE CUSTARD

1 large whole egg plus 1 large egg yolk

2 cups whole milk

½ cup sugar

¼ teaspoon kosher salt

½ cup semolina flour

1. Make the crust: Preheat oven to 325°F. Arrange ½-inch-thick layer of kataifi in the bottom and up and over the sides of a 9-inch pie dish (it will shrink during baking); brush gently all over with melted butter. Bake until golden, about 25 minutes.

2. Make the caramelized apples: Melt butter in a large high-sided skillet over medium-high heat. Add apple wedges and sugar. Cook, stirring occasionally, until apples are soft and caramelized, about 40 minutes. Transfer apples to a medium bowl.

3. Make the caramel: Add sugar to skillet, and cook, swirling pan occasionally, over high heat until sugar dissolves and turns medium amber, about 6 minutes. Remove skillet from heat. Slowly and carefully stir in cream (it will bubble and steam as you add it) until blended.

4. Cover bottom of crust with ¾ cup caramelized apples. Drizzle apples with 2 tablespoons caramel.

5. Make the custard: Whisk together egg and yolk in a medium bowl. Bring milk, sugar, and salt to a simmer in a medium saucepan over medium heat. Gradually add semolina flour, whisking constantly, until mixture starts to bubble, about 30 seconds. Remove from heat, and slowly whisk a third of semolina mixture into egg mixture. Whisk semolina-egg mixture into saucepan. Cook, whisking constantly, until thick, about 30 seconds.

6. Pour custard over caramelized apples in crust. Let stand at room temperature until set, about 1 hour. Top with remaining caramelized apples just before serving. Drizzle top of pie with some caramel (reheat if needed). Serve immediately.

POLENTA GRAPE SNACKING CAKE

The candy-like sweetness of the grape makes the fruit an ideal baking ingredient, especially the red varieties. Choose grapes that are in healthy clusters, plump, and ready to burst. Here, they are reined in by the savory flavors of rosemary and polenta for an ultra-satisfying snacking cake. **SERVES 12**

1 stick (½ cup) unsalted butter, plus more for pan

1½ cups unbleached all-purpose flour

½ cup quick-cooking polenta

1 teaspoon baking powder

¾ teaspoon kosher salt

½ cup granulated sugar

¼ cup honey

2 large eggs, room temperature

⅔ cup whole milk, room temperature

2 cups red seedless grapes

1 tablespoon whole fresh rosemary leaves

2 teaspoons sanding sugar or granulated sugar, for sprinkling

1. Preheat oven to 350°F. Brush bottom and sides of an 8-inch square baking pan with butter. Line bottom and two sides with parchment, leaving a 2-inch overhang; butter parchment.

2. Melt butter in a small saucepan over medium heat. Simmer, swirling pan occasionally, until butter turns golden brown and nutty-smelling, 8 to 10 minutes. Transfer to a small bowl to cool completely. Meanwhile, in a medium bowl, whisk together flour, polenta, baking powder, and salt.

3. In a large bowl, with an electric mixer on medium-high speed, beat cooled butter, granulated sugar, and honey until mixture resembles a sandy paste, 2 to 3 minutes. Beat in eggs, one at a time, beating well after each addition and scraping down sides of bowl as necessary. Reduce speed to low and beat in flour mixture in two batches, alternating with milk and beginning and ending with the flour, just until combined (do not overmix). Fold in 1 cup grapes.

4. Pour batter into prepared pan, smoothing top with an offset spatula. Bake 15 minutes. Scatter remaining 1 cup grapes, the rosemary, and sanding sugar over top. Bake until golden and a cake tester comes out clean, 30 to 35 minutes. Transfer pan to a wire rack to cool 15 minutes; remove cake using parchment overhang and cool completely on rack before serving.

APPLE–DATE BETTY

A Betty is a simple, homey dessert similar to a spiced crisp or cobbler but with diced or crumbled bread mixed with the fruit, to absorb the juices and form a hearty, satisfying treat. Top with heavy cream (or whipped cream or ice cream) before digging in. **SERVES 6**

5 slices country
white sandwich bread,
cut into ¾-inch pieces

6 tablespoons
unsalted butter, melted

¾ cup sugar

6 tablespoons apple cider

5 large Granny Smith
apples (about 2½ pounds
total), peeled, cored, and
cut into ¾-inch pieces

¾ cup chopped
dates, preferably
Medjool (4 ounces)

4 teaspoons unbleached
all-purpose flour

1 tablespoon
fresh lemon juice

Pinch of kosher salt

¼ teaspoon
ground allspice

Heavy cream, for serving

1. Preheat oven to 375°F. Scatter bread on a rimmed baking sheet and bake until dry and light golden brown, about 12 minutes, tossing halfway through. Crush half the bread to make crumbs, if desired. In a large bowl, combine butter, ¼ cup sugar, and 3 tablespoons cider, then stir in bread pieces and crumbs.

2. In another large bowl, combine apples, dates, flour, lemon juice, salt, allspice, and remaining ½ cup sugar and 3 tablespoons cider. Stir in ½ cup bread mixture. Transfer to an 8-inch square baking dish and top with remaining bread mixture. Cover with parchment-lined foil and bake until bubbling in center, 40 to 55 minutes. Uncover and bake until top is golden, 5 minutes more. Let cool 15 minutes (or let sit at room temperature up to 8 hours). To serve, divide among bowls and top with cream.

CINNAMON-SWIRL APPLE SLAB PIE

At first glance, this dessert calls to mind a tray of cinnamon rolls. The reality is even better: a party-size apple pie with a mix of sweet and tart fruit, topped with fragrant pâte brisée pinwheels. Bake any extra rounds on a parchment-lined baking sheet until very golden, about 12 minutes, for nibbling. **SERVES 16**

3 tablespoons unbleached all-purpose flour, plus more for dusting

2 recipes Pâte Brisée (page 236), each shaped into a rectangle

4 tablespoons unsalted butter, room temperature, plus 2 tablespoons, cold and cut into small cubes

½ cup packed light-brown sugar

1 teaspoon ground cinnamon

½ teaspoon kosher salt

4 pounds assorted apples (12 to 13 medium), such as Jonagold, Cortland, Granny Smith, and Empire, peeled, halved, cored, and cut into ¼-inch slices

2 tablespoons fresh lemon juice

6 tablespoons granulated sugar

1 teaspoon vanilla extract

1 large egg, lightly beaten, for egg wash

Fine sanding sugar, for sprinkling

1. On a lightly floured piece of parchment, roll one dough into a 12-by-17-inch rectangle. Transfer to a 10½-by-15¼-inch rimmed baking sheet or jelly-roll pan and press into bottom and up sides. Fold under edges of piecrust. Use excess dough to patch any holes. Refrigerate 30 minutes.

2. In a small bowl, combine room-temperature butter, brown sugar, cinnamon, and ¼ teaspoon salt. On a lightly floured piece of parchment, roll second dough into a 12-by-16-inch rectangle. Using an offset spatula, evenly spread butter mixture over dough, all the way to edges. Starting at a long end, tightly roll dough into a log. Transfer to a baking sheet and refrigerate until firm, about 30 minutes.

3. Preheat oven to 425°F with a rack in lower third and a foil-lined baking sheet on a rack below. In a large bowl, toss together apples, lemon juice, granulated sugar, flour, remaining ¼ teaspoon salt, and vanilla. Fill piecrust with apple mixture and dot with cold butter.

4. Cut dough log into ¼-inch slices (you'll have 64), rotating log occasionally to keep the slices round. Arrange slices, slightly overlapping, to cover apple mixture. Refrigerate until firm, about 30 minutes. Brush top of pie with egg wash and sprinkle with sanding sugar. Bake until top crust is just set, 20 minutes. Reduce temperature to 375°F and continue baking until crust is golden brown and juices are bubbling, about 1 hour. Transfer to a wire rack to cool completely. (Slab pie tastes best the day it's made but can be refrigerated up to 5 days.)

TIP:
You can poach
quince up to a
week in advance,
storing it in its
liquid; the longer it
marinates,
the pinker it gets.

QUINCE COBBLER

Take the humble cobbler up a notch: Slices of quince are cooked in a warm bath of maple and vanilla until tender and sweet, then baked under mounds of cornmeal-spiked biscuit dough. An opening in the center of the topping lets steam escape and reveals the bubbling, rosy-hued filling. **SERVES 8**

FOR THE FILLING

1 cup pure maple syrup

½ cup granulated sugar

5 quinces, peeled, cored, and quartered

1 vanilla bean, split and seeds scraped, pod reserved

2 teaspoons cornstarch

FOR THE TOPPING

1¾ cups unbleached all-purpose flour

⅓ cup fine yellow cornmeal

⅓ cup granulated sugar

2 teaspoons baking powder

¾ teaspoon kosher salt

1½ sticks (¾ cup) cold unsalted butter, cut into small pieces

1 cup heavy cream

3 tablespoons sliced almonds

Confectioners' sugar, for dusting

Whipped Cream (page 246), for serving

1. Make the filling: In a large pot, bring 5 cups water, the maple syrup, granulated sugar, quinces, and vanilla seeds and pod to a simmer over medium heat. Cover with a round of parchment, pressing it directly onto surface of quinces (for how-tos, see page 244). Cook until quinces are soft and rosy pink, about 2 hours. Discard vanilla pod.

2. Make the topping: Preheat oven to 375°F. In a medium bowl, sift together flour, cornmeal, granulated sugar, baking powder, and salt. Cut in butter with a pastry blender or rub in with your fingers until mixture resembles coarse meal with some large pieces remaining. Make a well in the center. Pour in cream and stir until combined.

3. Using a slotted spoon, transfer quinces to a medium bowl. Add 1 cup poaching liquid and the cornstarch and toss to combine. (Reserve remaining poaching liquid for another use.) Pour quinces with juices into a 9-inch deep-dish pie plate. Arrange large spoonfuls of topping mixture around outer edge of pie plate, leaving a space in the center. Sprinkle almonds over topping and bake until liquid is bubbling and topping is golden, about 50 minutes. Let cool completely. Using a fine-mesh sieve, dust with confectioners' sugar and serve with whipped cream.

APPLE HONEY UPSIDE-DOWN CAKE

The apples you snack on or cook into applesauce are not the same ones you want for this pretty-as-it-is-delectable dessert. Choose varieties that are firm (like Winesap, Mutsu, or Granny Smith) so they'll maintain their shape when baked and inverted onto a serving plate, and that have enough tartness to counter the buttery-sweet caramel. **SERVES 8 TO 10**

Vegetable oil cooking spray

1½ cups unbleached all-purpose flour

1½ teaspoons baking powder

1 teaspoon kosher salt

1⅓ cups sugar

⅓ cup honey

2 large eggs

1 stick (½ cup) unsalted butter, melted, plus 4 tablespoons, room temperature

¼ cup whole milk

3 firm tart apples, such as Mutsu, Winesap, or Granny Smith, peeled, cored, and cut into ½-inch-thick wedges

1. Preheat oven to 350°F. Spray a 9-inch round cake pan with oil. In a medium bowl, whisk together flour, baking powder, and salt. In another medium bowl, whisk together ⅔ cup sugar, the honey, eggs, melted butter, and milk. Whisk egg mixture into flour mixture until just combined.

2. In a small heavy saucepan over high heat, combine remaining ⅔ cup sugar and 3 tablespoons water. Cook, swirling pan occasionally (do not stir), until sugar mixture is deep amber, about 5 minutes. Remove from heat and stir in room-temperature butter. Immediately pour into prepared pan.

3. Decoratively arrange layers of apples over caramel filling. Spread batter evenly over apples. Bake until top springs back when lightly touched, 45 to 55 minutes. Loosen edges with a knife. Let stand 5 minutes before inverting onto a serving plate. Serve warm or at room temperature.

TIP:
This dough recipe makes two disks, and you'll only need one for this dish; you can freeze the other—it will keep well for up to 3 months. Thaw overnight in the refrigerator before using.

PEAR AND FIG PANDOWDY

This deep-dish dessert with the funny name is loaded with homey autumnal appeal. Apples are traditional, but pears and figs offer a sophisticated flavor twist—as does the hazelnut-infused patchwork crust. Try serving it with a salty, creamy cheese, such as Gorgonzola or another favorite blue. **SERVES 8**

FOR THE CRUST

1 ¾ cups unbleached all-purpose flour, plus more for dusting

½ cup blanched hazelnuts, toasted (page 246) and ground

1 teaspoon granulated sugar

1 teaspoon kosher salt

2 sticks (1 cup) cold unsalted butter, cut into small pieces

¼ to ½ cup ice-cold water

1 large egg

1 tablespoon heavy cream

Fine sanding sugar, for sprinkling

FOR THE FILLING

4 pounds firm pears, such as Bosc or Bartlett, peeled, cored, and cut into ½-inch wedges

⅓ cup granulated sugar

¼ cup chopped dried figs

2 tablespoons lemon juice

1 tablespoon unbleached all-purpose flour

½ teaspoon ground cinnamon

Pinch of freshly grated nutmeg

1. Make the crust: Pulse flour, hazelnuts, granulated sugar, and salt in a food processor until just combined. Add butter and pulse until mixture resembles coarse meal, with a few pea-size pieces of butter remaining. With machine running, slowly add ¼ cup ice water and process until mixture just begins to hold together. If dough is too dry, add up to another ¼ cup water, 1 tablespoon at a time, and pulse; don't overmix. Divide dough in half, pat each half into a disk, and wrap in plastic. Refrigerate 1 disk until firm, about 1 hour. (Freeze remaining disk, up to 3 months, for another use; thaw in refrigerator before using.)

2. Preheat oven to 375°F. Roll out dough to a ⅛-inch-thick rectangle on a lightly floured surface. Transfer to a piece of parchment. Cut dough into 2-by-3-inch pieces. Freeze until firm, about 30 minutes.

3. Make the filling: Combine pears, granulated sugar, figs, lemon juice, flour, cinnamon, and nutmeg in a large bowl. Transfer filling to an 8-by-11-inch baking dish.

4. Arrange dough pieces on top in a patchwork design, overlapping slightly and leaving holes in between as steam vents. In a small bowl, whisk together egg and heavy cream. Brush dough with egg wash and sprinkle with sanding sugar. Bake until top is golden brown and filling is bubbling in the center, about 55 minutes. Transfer to a wire rack to cool 15 minutes before serving.

RUFFLED PUMPKIN MILK PIE

Upgrade your standby pumpkin pie with this frilly version—a squash-imbued twist on a classic Greek custard pie in which spirals of crispy phyllo replace a standard crust. The pastry sheets are loosely rumpled by hand, any imperfections disappearing in the final, baked result. **SERVES 6 TO 8**

8 tablespoons (½ cup) clarified butter or ghee, melted

14 to 18 sheets store-bought phyllo (14-by-18-inch sheets), thawed if frozen

6 large eggs

¾ cup pure pumpkin purée

1 cup whole milk

½ cup heavy cream

¾ cup granulated sugar

1 teaspoon vanilla extract

½ teaspoon freshly ground cardamom

¼ teaspoon ground cinnamon

¼ teaspoon kosher salt

Confectioners' sugar, for dusting

1. Preheat oven to 350°F. Lightly brush a 9-inch round cake pan with clarified butter. Line pan with a 13-inch parchment round; brush parchment with more clarified butter.

2. Place 1 sheet of phyllo dough on work surface with one long side parallel to edge of work surface. Lightly brush phyllo with clarified butter. Using your hands, loosely ruffle phyllo by pushing long sides toward each other to create a long accordion shape about 1½ to 2 inches tall. Place upright in center of prepared cake pan, folding around to create a spiral. Repeat process with remaining sheets, continuing the spiral outward until bottom of pan is covered. Brush remaining clarified butter over tops phyllo ruffles in pan. Bake until golden brown, 25 to 30 minutes. Transfer pan to a wire rack to cool while you make the filling (leave oven on).

3. In a large bowl, whisk eggs, pumpkin purée, milk, cream, granulated sugar, vanilla, cardamom, cinnamon, and salt until smooth. Transfer mixture to a measuring cup or pitcher. Gradually pour over baked phyllo, evenly covering surface. Return pan to oven and bake until filling is set, 35 to 45 minutes. Transfer to a wire rack to cool completely. Using parchment, lift pie out of pan; carefully remove parchment and transfer to a platter. Dust with confectioners' sugar and serve.

TIP:
Clarified butter and ghee have the milk solids removed, so they have a higher smoke point than butter and work nicely with phyllo dough. They can be found at many markets, but feel free to use melted butter if you prefer.

CRANBERRY MERINGUE TARTLETS

A brown-butter press-in crust forms a mellow counterpoint for these tangy, cranberry-orange-custard tarts. Chill them well before piping on a constellation of creamy, whipped meringue swirls to finish. Serve as is or lightly toast the meringue to dreamy perfection. **SERVES 6**

FOR THE CRUST

1½ sticks (¾ cup) unsalted butter, cut into pieces

1½ teaspoons vanilla extract

1½ cups unbleached all-purpose flour

¾ teaspoon baking powder

¼ cup sugar

¼ teaspoon kosher salt

FOR THE FILLING

3½ cups (12 ounces) fresh or thawed frozen cranberries

⅔ cup fresh orange juice (from about 3 oranges)

½ teaspoon kosher salt

1½ cups sugar

4 tablespoons unsalted butter, cut into pieces

1 large whole egg plus 2 large egg yolks (reserve whites for topping)

FOR THE TOPPING

2 large egg whites, room temperature

½ cup sugar

1. Make the crust: Preheat oven to 350°F. In a small saucepan, melt butter over medium heat. Continue to cook, stirring frequently, until deep golden brown, 5 to 8 minutes. Let cool to room temperature, about 10 minutes. Stir in vanilla. In a medium bowl, whisk together flour, baking powder, sugar, and salt. Pour brown butter mixture into flour mixture and stir just until combined. Divide dough among six 4-inch tart pans with removable bottoms; pat into bottoms and up sides. Arrange tart pans on a rimmed baking sheet. Refrigerate until firm, about 1 hour. With a fork, pierce bottom of each tart shell all over. Line with parchment and fill with pie weights or dried beans. Bake until edges are golden, about 20 minutes. Remove weights and parchment and continue baking until crust is golden, about 8 minutes more. Transfer to a wire rack to cool completely.

2. Make the filling: In a medium pan over medium-high, bring cranberries, orange juice, ½ cup water, and the salt to a boil. Reduce to medium, cover, and simmer, stirring occasionally, until berries are very soft, 10 to 15 minutes. Strain through a fine-mesh sieve (you should have about 1½ cups); discard solids. Return mixture to pan. Add sugar and cook over medium-high, stirring, until sugar is dissolved. Add butter and whisk until melted. In a heatproof bowl, whisk whole egg and yolks. Gradually whisk in half of hot cranberry mixture, then pour back into pan. Place over medium heat and simmer, stirring constantly, until mixture coats the back of a wooden spoon, about 8 minutes. Strain through a fine-mesh sieve into a heatproof measuring cup; pour into tart shells. Press plastic wrap directly on surface of curd and refrigerate until cold, at least 2 hours and up to overnight.

3. Make the topping: Whisk together egg whites and sugar in a heat-proof bowl set over (not in) a pot of simmering water until mixture is warm to the touch and no longer feels grainy when rubbed between two fingers. Remove from heat and beat on medium-high speed until stiff, glossy peaks form, about 6 minutes. Transfer meringue into a piping bag fitted with a ½-inch tip and pipe swirls onto tartlets.

WINTER

Quickest way to banish thoughts of frosty winds and short days? Tropical fruits, and the wondrous desserts they inspire. Bright, bracing, and carrying promises of sunshine— they're all the antidote you need.

CITRUS FLAN

The classic Spanish custard gets a fresh update with the addition of orange zest–plus sections of juicy orange and grapefruit that mingle with the caramel on the serving platter. It's an elegant, bright (and make-ahead) finish for a gratifying meal. **SERVES 6 TO 8**

1½ cups sugar

4 cups whole milk

Zest of 2 oranges, removed in strips with a peeler (save the oranges for step 6)

5 large whole eggs plus 5 large egg yolks

¾ teaspoon kosher salt

1 teaspoon vanilla extract

4 large navel oranges, peel and pith removed, citrus removed in segments (page 246)

2 ruby red grapefruits, peel and pith removed, citrus removed in segments (page 246)

1. Preheat oven to 325°F, with a rack in center of oven. Place a 9-inch cake pan in a large roasting pan. Bring a large kettle or pot of water to a boil.

2. Make the caramel: In a small saucepan over medium-high heat, mix ½ cup sugar and 3 tablespoons water, stirring to combine. Do not stir again. Cook, washing down the sides of the pan with a pastry brush dipped in water, or covering with a tight-fitting lid, to prevent crystals from forming, until caramel is amber, about 8 minutes, swirling pan to color evenly. Carefully pour into cake pan, swirling to coat bottom evenly.

3. Make the custard: In a medium saucepan, heat milk, ½ cup sugar, and the orange zest over medium heat and cook, stirring occasionally just until mixture bubbles around the edges and sugar dissolves, about 5 to 7 minutes (do not let it boil). Remove from heat.

4. In a large bowl, whisk together eggs, yolks, remaining ½ cup of sugar, and the salt. While whisking, gradually pour in hot milk mixture. Strain through a fine-mesh sieve into a large measuring cup or a bowl. Stir in vanilla.

5. Pour custard into cake pan. Transfer to oven and pour enough boiling water into roasting pan to come halfway up sides of cake pan. Bake until custard is just set, about 50 to 60 minutes. (The center of the custard should tremble slightly when gently shaken.)

6. Remove roasting pan from oven. Using tongs, carefully remove cake pan from hot water bath and transfer to a wire rack to cool 1 hour. Cover with plastic wrap and refrigerate until well chilled, at least 8 hours and up to 3 days. To serve, run a sharp knife or offset spatula around edge of flan. Place a large rimmed serving plate upside down over top of cake pan. Invert and gently remove cake pan. Arrange citrus segments on platter around flan, letting juices naturally combine with caramel. Slice and serve.

KEY LIME CREAM PUFFS

Fans of the lip-puckering goodness of Key lime pie and the easy elegance of cream puffs will be charmed by these bite-sized beauties. Pipe in the filling gently, until each puff is full but not bursting. Set out a plate with afternoon tea and watch them disappear. **MAKES ABOUT 24**

FOR THE KEY LIME CURD

1/2 cup sugar

2 tablespoons cornstarch

1/4 teaspoon kosher salt

1 large whole egg plus
2 large egg yolks

2 teaspoons finely grated Key lime zest plus 2/3 cup fresh juice (from about 12 Key limes)

2/3 cup sweetened condensed milk (from one 14.5-ounce can)

2 tablespoons unsalted butter

1/2 cup cold heavy cream

FOR THE CREAM PUFFS

1 stick (1/2 cup) unsalted butter

1 teaspoon sugar

1/2 teaspoon kosher salt

1 1/4 cups unbleached all-purpose flour

4 large eggs, room temperature, plus 1 large egg, lightly beaten, for brushing

Key Lime Glaze (page 246)

1. Make the curd: In a medium saucepan, whisk together sugar, cornstarch, and salt. Whisk in egg and yolks, then lime zest and juice. Bring to a boil over medium-high heat. Cook, whisking constantly, 1 minute. Whisk in condensed milk and return to a boil. Remove from heat and strain through a fine-mesh sieve. Whisk in butter until combined. Cover with plastic wrap, pressing directly onto surface. Refrigerate until set, at least 3 hours and up to overnight. In a medium bowl, whisk heavy cream to stiff peaks. Whisk chilled curd to loosen, then whisk in half the whipped cream. Fold in remaining cream. Refrigerate until chilled, about 1 hour or up to overnight.

2. Make the cream puffs: Preheat oven to 450°F, with a rack in upper and bottom thirds. Line 2 baking sheets with parchment or nonstick baking mats. In a medium saucepan, bring butter, sugar, salt, and 1 cup water to a boil. Remove from heat and, with a wooden spoon, immediately stir in flour. Cook over medium-high, stirring constantly, until mixture pulls away from sides of pan, about 3 minutes. With an electric mixer, beat on low until slightly cooled, about 2 minutes. Add 4 eggs, one at a time, beating until incorporated. (When dough is ready, a soft peak will form when you touch the dough and pull your finger away. If it doesn't, add the lightly beaten egg, a teaspoon at a time, until batter is smooth and shiny.) Transfer dough to a pastry bag fitted with 1/2-inch plain tip (such as Ateco #806). Pipe into rounds about 1 1/2 inches in diameter and 3/4 inch high. Smooth peaks with a wet finger, rounding tops. Brush with remaining egg wash. Reduce oven to 350°F and bake until golden brown, 25 to 30 minutes. Transfer pans to wires racks to cool completely.

3. Assemble: Set a wire rack on a rimmed baking sheet. Dip top of each cooled cream puff into Key lime glaze and place on prepared sheet to set, at least 30 minutes. Fill a pastry bag fitted with a 1/2-inch plain tip (such as Ateco #806) with chilled Key lime curd. Insert tip into bottom of each cream puff and fill.

BANANA CREAM PIE

Some things are classics for a reason. And piled high with homemade vanilla pudding, whipped cream, and slices of ripe but firm bananas, this pie answers that call. The graham cracker crust is pre-baked, filled, then chilled, so the pie is easy to make ahead—add the whipped cream topping just before serving. **SERVES 10**

FOR THE CRUST

1¼ cups graham cracker crumbs (from about 10 crackers)

¼ cup sugar

4 tablespoons unsalted butter, melted

FOR THE FILLING

4 cups cold heavy cream

1½ cups whole milk

1½ cups plus 2 teaspoons sugar

1 vanilla bean, split and seeds scraped, pod reserved

2 large whole eggs plus 3 large egg yolks

½ cup cornstarch

3 pounds firm but ripe bananas (6 to 7), peeled and cut crosswise into ¼-inch-thick slices on the bias

½ teaspoon vanilla extract

1. Make the crust: Preheat oven to 350°F. In a medium bowl, combine graham cracker crumbs and sugar. Add melted butter and mix well. Press mixture firmly into a 9-inch pie pan using the bottom of a dry measuring cup. Bake until browned, about 25 minutes. Transfer to a wire rack to cool 15 minutes.

2. Make the filling: In a large heavy-bottomed saucepan over medium heat, combine 2 cups cream, the milk, ½ cup sugar, and the vanilla pod and seeds. Bring to a gentle boil, whisking to dissolve sugar. Remove from heat; discard vanilla pod.

3. In a medium bowl, combine whole eggs, egg yolks, cornstarch, and 1 cup sugar. Whisk until pale yellow. Drizzle 1 cup hot cream mixture into egg yolk mixture, whisking constantly. Gradually add egg mixture to hot cream mixture, whisking constantly. Return pan to medium heat and bring to a simmer, stirring constantly with a wooden spoon until thickened, about 5 minutes. Strain through a fine-mesh sieve into a clean bowl. Cover with plastic wrap, pressing directly onto surface. Refrigerate until chilled, about 4 hours.

4. To assemble: Spread ½ cup custard over bottom of prepared crust, smoothing with the back of a large spoon. Arrange banana slices (not quite one-third) in a tight, tiled pattern over custard, pressing down to pack firmly. Repeat to build a second layer, using ¾ cup custard and enough bananas to cover. For third layer, spread ¾ cup custard and top with remaining bananas, starting 1 inch from outer edge and working toward center. Spread 1 cup custard evenly over bananas. Cover with plastic wrap and chill at least 4 hours or overnight.

5. In a medium bowl, whip remaining 2 cups heavy cream until soft peaks form. Add remaining 2 teaspoons sugar and the vanilla extract, and continue to whip until stiff peaks form. Using a flexible spatula, spread whipped cream over pie. Serve immediately.

DEEP-DISH DRIED-APPLE AND CRANBERRY PIE

Dried fruit is an excellent way to savor your favorites past their season. Here, chewy, almost candy-like apple rings offer deep, concentrated flavor. Cider brings them back to life—as do cooked-to-bursting cranberries. **SERVES 12**

FOR THE CRUST

2 cups unbleached all-purpose flour, plus more for dusting

1½ teaspoons kosher salt

1 tablespoon granulated sugar

1½ sticks cold unsalted butter, cut into pieces

1 tablespoon apple-cider vinegar

2 to 4 tablespoons ice-cold water

FOR THE FILLING

10 ounces dried apple rings

4 cups apple cider

½ cup light-brown sugar

1 cinnamon stick

¼ teaspoon kosher salt

12 ounces fresh or thawed frozen cranberries

3 tablespoons unbleached all-purpose flour

⅓ cup granulated sugar

FOR THE TOPPING

½ cup unbleached all-purpose flour

⅓ cup old-fashioned oats

⅓ cup light-brown sugar

¼ teaspoon kosher salt

5 tablespoons unsalted butter, room temperature

1. Make the crust: Pulse flour, salt, and granulated sugar in a food processor to combine. Add butter and pulse until mixture resembles coarse meal, with a few pea-size pieces of butter remaining. Whisk together vinegar and 2 tablespoons ice water in a small bowl. Drizzle over flour mixture; pulse until mixture just begins to hold together when pinched. If dough is too dry, add up to 2 tablespoons more ice water, 1 tablespoon at a time, and pulse. (Don't overmix.) Transfer dough to a piece of plastic wrap, cover, and press into a disk. Refrigerate until firm, at least 30 minutes or up to 1 day.

2. Roll out dough to a 13-inch round on a lightly floured work surface. Press into bottom and up sides of a 9-inch springform pan. Trim dough flush with rim, using excess to patch any cracks or holes in crust. Refrigerate until firm, at least 30 minutes or up to 1 day.

3. Make the filling: In a large saucepan over medium-high heat bring dried apples, cider, brown sugar, cinnamon, and salt to a boil. Cover, reduce heat to medium, and boil, stirring occasionally, until apples are tender, 12 to 15 minutes. Stir in cranberries and boil, uncovered, just until berries begin to burst, 3 to 4 minutes. Drain, reserving liquid. Transfer apple mixture to a bowl; discard cinnamon. Return liquid to pan; boil until reduced to ⅔ cup, 8 to 10 minutes. Toss with apple mixture. Let cool, then stir in flour and granulated sugar.

4. Make the topping: In a medium bowl, combine flour, oats, brown sugar, and salt. Using your fingers, rub butter into flour mixture until large pieces form and no dry flour remains. Refrigerate, covered, until firm, about 20 minutes.

5. Preheat oven to 375°F. Place piecrust on a foil-lined rimmed baking sheet. Pour filling into crust. Break topping into large pieces and sprinkle over filling. Bake until filling is bubbling and crust is golden brown, 1 hour to 1 hour 15 minutes. (If crust is browning too quickly, tent with foil.) Transfer to a wire rack to cool completely before removing outer ring from pan and serving.

TIP:
To make this even
simpler, you can use
lightly sweetened
whipped cream
instead of meringue.
The tart shell can be
baked up to two days
ahead; store at
room temperature.

MEYER LEMON TART

One of our food editors, Lauryn, who grew up with a Meyer lemon tree in her Los Angeles backyard, cooked up this citrusy dessert to remind her of home. A gluten-free hazelnut crust is first blind-baked, then teamed with a lemon curd filling and a wreath of toasted meringue. **SERVES 8 TO 10**

FOR THE CRUST

1⅓ cups blanched hazelnuts, toasted

¼ cup confectioners' sugar, sifted

2 tablespoons cornstarch

½ teaspoon kosher salt

1 large egg white

2 tablespoons unsalted butter, room temperature

FOR THE FILLING

½ teaspoon unflavored powdered gelatin

2 teaspoons cold water

⅔ cup granulated sugar

1 tablespoon finely grated Meyer lemon zest plus ⅔ cup fresh juice (from 3 Meyer lemons)

8 large egg yolks (reserve 2 whites for meringue)

¼ teaspoon kosher salt

1 stick (½ cup) plus 2 tablespoons cold unsalted butter, cut into pieces

FOR THE MERINGUE

2 large egg whites

½ cup granulated sugar

Pinch of cream of tartar

Pinch of kosher salt

½ teaspoon vanilla extract

1. Make the crust: Preheat oven to 375°F. Pulse hazelnuts in a food processor until finely ground. Add confectioners' sugar, cornstarch, and salt and pulse to combine. Add egg white and butter and process until dough comes together. Transfer ⅔ cup dough to the bottom of a 9-inch fluted tart pan with a removable bottom. With an offset spatula or the back of a spoon, spread and press it into an even layer. Press remaining ⅓ cup dough firmly up sides of pan. Freeze until firm, about 15 minutes. Remove from freezer and pierce all over with the tines of a fork. Bake until golden brown and dry, 20 to 25 minutes (if browning too quickly, tent edges with foil). Transfer to a wire rack to cool completely. (The tart shell can be baked up to 2 days ahead; store at room temperature.)

2. Make the filling: In a small bowl, sprinkle gelatin over cold water; let stand 5 minutes. Meanwhile, in a medium saucepan, off heat, whisk together granulated sugar, lemon zest and juice, egg yolks, and salt. Add butter and cook over medium, whisking constantly, until melted. Continue to cook until mixture is thick enough to coat the back of a spoon, 5 minutes more. Remove from heat and whisk in gelatin mixture. Strain through a fine-mesh sieve into a heatproof bowl; then pour into cooled crust. Refrigerate until filling has set, at least 2 hours.

3. Make the meringue: In the bowl of a mixer fitted with the whisk attachment, beat together egg whites, granulated sugar, cream of tartar, and salt. Place bowl over (not in) a saucepan of simmering water. Cook, whisking frequently, until mixture is warm to the touch and no longer feels grainy when rubbed between two fingers. Return bowl to mixer and whisk on high speed until stiff peaks form, about 5 minutes. Add vanilla and beat 1 minute more. Transfer meringue to a piping bag fitted with a large round tip (such as Ateco #808). Pipe large rounds around perimeter of tart. Before serving, use a kitchen torch to toast meringue, moving flame back and forth until evenly browned.

PINEAPPLE-BANANA UPSIDE-DOWN CAKE

It's unclear whom we have to thank for the caramelly goodness of upside-down cake, but cooking lore says that bakers have been flipping their cakes to reveal showstopping fruit toppings for centuries. In this version, a spiral of golden pineapple slices enhances a delicious banana cake. **SERVES 8 TO 10**

2 sticks (1 cup)
unsalted butter, melted

1 cup packed
light-brown sugar

½ large pineapple,
peeled, cut in half
lengthwise, cored, and
sliced crosswise into
⅛-inch-thick pieces

2 cups unbleached
all-purpose flour

1½ cups granulated sugar

1 teaspoon baking powder

½ teaspoon baking soda

1 teaspoon kosher salt

2 very ripe bananas,
mashed until smooth
(about 1 cup)

½ cup buttermilk

3 large eggs,
room temperature

2 teaspoons
vanilla extract

1. Preheat oven to 350°F. Pour ¼ cup melted butter into a 9-inch round baking pan, swirling to evenly coat bottom. Sprinkle brown sugar evenly over butter. To create a flower motif: Arrange pineapple, with rounded edges facing outward, over brown sugar; overlap slices in concentric circle from the center out, to completely cover cake.

2. In a medium bowl, whisk flour, granulated sugar, baking powder, baking soda, and salt until combined.

3. In a large bowl, whisk remaining ¾ cup melted butter, the bananas, buttermilk, eggs, and vanilla until well combined. Add flour mixture and stir to combine. Pour cake batter over pineapples, smoothing top with a small offset spatula.

4. Bake until top is deep golden and a cake tester comes out clean, about 1 hour 15 minutes. Transfer pan to a wire rack to cool 15 minutes. Run a knife around edges of pan, invert cake onto a plate, and let cool completely before serving.

TIP:
When cutting a pineapple, begin by slicing off the top and bottom. Stand it on end and, slicing downward, cut the skin off in wide strips. With your knife, carve out the eyes. Then halve, core, and cut the fruit crosswise into ⅛-inch-thick slices.

COCONUT LAYER CAKE

This impressive confection starts with a simple vanilla cake, but the layers contain treasures: rich, coconut custard, sliced kiwis, and strawberry-infused whipped cream. It gets all wrapped up in blushing pink frosting and a coating of snowy coconut. If you don't have vanilla bean, simply double the vanilla extract. **SERVES 8 TO 10**

FOR THE CAKE

1½ sticks (¾ cup) unsalted butter, room temperature, plus more for pan

1½ cups granulated sugar

2¼ teaspoons baking powder

1½ teaspoons kosher salt

2 large whole eggs plus 2 large yolks, room temperature

1 vanilla bean, split and seeds scraped

1 teaspoon vanilla extract

2¼ cups unbleached all-purpose flour

¾ cup whole milk, room temperature

FOR THE CUSTARD FILLING

¼ cup plus 2 tablespoons granulated sugar

3 tablespoons cornstarch

¼ teaspoon kosher salt

3 large egg yolks (save the whites for the frosting)

1½ cups whole milk

1 tablespoon unsalted butter

2 tablespoons virgin coconut oil, melted

1 cup sweetened shredded coconut

1¼ cups cold heavy cream

1 tablespoon crushed freeze-dried strawberries

6 kiwis, peeled and thinly sliced

FOR THE FROSTING

3 large egg whites, room temperature

1 cup packed light-brown sugar

¼ teaspoon cream of tartar

½ teaspoon vanilla extract

Pink gel-paste food coloring, such as AmeriColor Dusty Rose (optional)

2 cups sweetened shredded coconut

1. Make the cake: Preheat oven to 350°F. Butter two 8-inch round cake pans. Combine butter, sugar, baking powder, and salt in the bowl of an electric mixer fitted with paddle attachment. Beat on medium speed until light and fluffy, about 3 minutes. Add whole eggs and yolks, one at a time, beating to combine well after each addition. Beat in vanilla seeds and extract. Add flour in three batches, alternating with milk and beginning and ending with flour, beating until just combined.

2. Divide batter between prepared pans, smoothing tops with a small offset spatula. Bake until a cake tester inserted in center comes out with a few crumbs attached, 35 to 40 minutes. Transfer pans to a wire rack to cool 15 minutes; turn cakes out to cool completely, at least 30 minutes or, tightly wrapped in plastic, up to overnight.

(continued)

3. Make the custard filling: In a small saucepan (off heat), whisk together sugar, cornstarch, and salt. Whisk in egg yolks, then milk. Place over medium-high heat and bring to a boil, whisking constantly. Continue to cook 1 minute more, whisking. Remove from heat and pour through a fine-mesh sieve into a heatproof bowl. Whisk in butter and coconut oil. Cover with plastic wrap, pressing directly onto surface to prevent a skin from forming. Refrigerate until chilled, at least 2 hours and up to 2 days.

4. Assemble: Whisk custard to lighten. Stir in shredded coconut. In a medium bowl, whip heavy cream to stiff peaks. Fold 1¼ cups whipped cream into coconut custard. Fold crushed berries into remaining whipped cream.

TIP:
To split cake layers evenly, after leveling, measure the layer's height and insert toothpicks at the halfway point, all the way around. Use a long, serrated knife and a gentle sawing motion to cut just above the toothpicks.

5. With a serrated knife, trim tops of cakes to level; split each cake horizontally to form a total of 4 layers. Place one layer on a cake round. Spread 1 cup coconut custard over cake. Top with half of kiwis in an even layer. Top with a generous ½ cup coconut custard then a second cake layer. Spread evenly with berry whipped cream. Top with a third cake layer. Layer with remaining custard and kiwis. Top with final cake layer. Refrigerate at least 2 hours and, tightly wrapped in plastic, up to overnight.

6. Make the frosting: Combine egg whites, brown sugar, and cream of tartar with 5 tablespoons cold water in a heatproof bowl set over (not in) a pot of simmering water. Whisk until sugar is dissolved and an instant-read thermometer reads 170°F, about 3 minutes. Remove from heat and transfer to a stand mixer fitted with the whisk attachment. Whisk on high until stiff peaks form and mixture is cool, 5 to 7 minutes; whisk in vanilla. If using, stir in food gel a few drops at a time until desired color is achieved. Cover cake evenly with frosting. Sprinkle coconut over top and sides. (Cake is best served on the day it's made but can be refrigerated, tightly wrapped, up to 2 days.)

ORANGE MARMALADE CAKE WITH ROASTED ORANGES

The much-loved combination of chocolate and orange meet in this sophisticated cake flavored by marmalade and fresh zest, with a dark chocolate frosting. Don't forget the slow-roasted orange slices. Arrange them overlapping in the center, or simply placed around the rim, to ensure every piece gets a garnish. **SERVES 8 TO 10**

FOR THE CAKE

2 sticks (1 cup) unsalted butter, room temperature, plus more for pans

1½ cups unbleached all-purpose flour, plus more for pans

1½ teaspoons baking powder

1 teaspoon kosher salt

1 cup plus 3 tablespoons granulated sugar

⅓ cup Orange Marmalade (see page 240)

1 tablespoon orange zest plus 1 orange, sliced into thin rounds

1 teaspoon vanilla extract

4 large eggs, room temperature

⅓ cup sour cream

FOR THE FROSTING

1¾ cups confectioners' sugar

½ cup unsweetened Dutch-process cocoa powder

1 stick (½ cup) unsalted butter, room temperature

¼ cup whole milk

1 teaspoon vanilla extract

¼ teaspoon kosher salt

1. Make the cake: Preheat oven to 325°F. Butter a 10-inch cake pan and line with parchment; butter parchment. In a medium bowl, whisk flour, baking powder, and salt until well combined. With an electric mixer on medium-high speed, beat butter and 1 cup granulated sugar until pale and fluffy, about 3 minutes. Beat in marmalade, orange zest, and vanilla until well combined, about 1 minute. Add eggs, one at a time, beating thoroughly after each and scraping down sides of the bowl as needed. Reduce speed to low and add flour mixture in 2 batches, alternating with sour cream and beating until just incorporated. Transfer batter to prepared pan, smoothing top with a small offset spatula. Bake until cake is golden and a cake tester inserted into center comes out clean, about 50 minutes. Transfer to a wire rack to cool completely. (Leave oven on, at 325°F, for roasting oranges.)

2. Arrange oranges slices in a single layer on a parchment-lined baking sheet and sprinkle generously with remaining 3 tablespoons sugar. Bake, turning once halfway through, until oranges are slightly caramelized and pith is tender, 45 to 50 minutes.

3. Make the frosting: Transfer cake to a platter or cake stand. Sift confectioners' sugar and cocoa powder into a large bowl. Add butter, milk, vanilla, and salt. Using an electric mixer, beat on medium-high speed until smooth and fluffy, about 4 minutes. Spread frosting over top of cooled cake, using an offset spatula to create a smooth finish or swirls. Arrange roasted oranges on cake, overlapping slices slightly, and serve.

ATLANTIC BEACH TART BARS

Bringing together the best qualities of lemon bars and Key lime pie, this creamy, tangy dessert is filled with lemon juice and condensed milk. The surprise is the press-in crust, made with just three ingredients—saltine crackers, butter, and sugar. It's lightly salty and mercifully uncomplicated. **SERVES 16**

Vegetable oil
cooking spray

7 ounces saltine
crackers (about 54)

1 stick (½ cup)
plus 5 tablespoons
unsalted butter, melted

¾ cup granulated sugar

1 large whole egg plus
2 large egg yolks

1 can (14 ounces)
sweetened condensed
milk (1¼ cups)

1 cup fresh lemon juice
(from 6 lemons)

¼ teaspoon kosher salt

Confectioners' sugar,
for dusting

1. Preheat oven to 350°F. Spray two 4-by-14-inch fluted-edge tart pans with removable bottoms with oil. In a food processor, pulse crackers until finely ground (you should have about 2¼ cups). Add butter and granulated sugar and pulse to combine. Divide mixture between pans and firmly press into bottoms and up sides. Bake until golden brown, 15 to 20 minutes.

2. In a medium bowl, whisk together egg and yolks. Whisk in condensed milk, lemon juice, and salt. Remove baked crusts from oven and carefully divide filling between pans. Return to oven and bake until set, 12 to 15 minutes.

3. Transfer to a wire rack to cool completely. Refrigerate until cold, at least 2 hours or up to overnight. Remove from pans and dust with confectioners' sugar. Cut into slices and serve.

TIP:
This recipe can also
be made in a 9-by-13-inch
rimmed baking sheet.
Line the sheet with
parchment after spraying,
leaving a 2-inch
overhang on the
long sides, and use the
overhangs to lift
out the chilled tart; then
cut into squares.

Clementine
Granita

Grapefruit–
Cardamom Granita

Lime–Lemongrass
Granita

GRANITA, THREE WAYS

A granita is just fruit juice and simple syrup (sugar and water), frozen and then scraped into spoonable crystals. But with some zingy flavors—a slice of ginger, a handful of herbs or spices—the icy treat takes on a decidedly grown-up appeal. **SERVES 4 TO 6**

CLEMENTINE GRANITA

¼ cup sugar

Pinch of kosher salt

1 slice (½ inch) peeled fresh ginger

2 cups freshly squeezed clementine or mandarin juice (from about 24 clementines)

1 tablespoon fresh lemon juice

In a small saucepan, bring sugar, ¼ cup water, the salt, and ginger to a boil, stirring, until sugar dissolves. Remove from heat and let cool 30 minutes, then discard ginger. Stir in clementine and lemon juices and transfer to a nonreactive 8-inch square baking dish. Freeze until solid, about 4 hours. Scrape granita with a fork to fluff.

LIME-LEMONGRASS GRANITA

½ cup sugar

Pinch of kosher salt

1 tablespoon finely minced lemongrass

2 cups freshly squeezed lime juice (from about 16 limes)

In a small saucepan, bring sugar, ¼ cup water, the salt, and minced lemongrass to a boil, stirring, until sugar dissolves. Remove from heat and let cool 30 minutes. Strain through a fine-mesh sieve into a medium bowl; discard lemongrass. Stir in lime juice and transfer to a nonreactive 8-inch square baking dish. Freeze until solid, about 4 hours. Scrape granita with a fork to fluff.

GRAPEFRUIT-CARDAMOM GRANITA

¼ cup sugar

Pinch of kosher salt

4 cardamom pods, crushed

2 cups freshly squeezed
grapefruit juice
(from about 3 grapefruits)

In a medium saucepan, bring sugar, ¼ cup water,
the salt, and crushed cardamom to a boil, stirring
until sugar dissolves. Remove from heat and let
cool 30 minutes. Strain through a fine-mesh sieve
over a large bowl; discard cardamom. Stir in
grapefruit juice and transfer to a nonreactive
9-by-13-inch baking dish. Freeze until solid, about
4 hours. Scrape granita with a fork to fluff.

CITRUS BUNDT

More than half a dozen lemons and oranges go into this glorious Bundt: three or four in the batter, three more in the syrup that soaks the warm cake, and one in the finishing glaze. Want to gild the lily? Top with some candied zest and serve with whipped cream. Absolute perfection. **SERVES 10 TO 12**

FOR THE CAKE

Vegetable oil
cooking spray

2¾ cups unbleached
all-purpose flour, plus
more for pan

2 medium lemons

1 large or 2 small oranges

1½ cups superfine sugar

2 teaspoons
baking powder

1¾ teaspoons kosher salt

¾ cup crème fraîche

6 large eggs, room
temperature

1½ sticks (¾ cup)
unsalted butter, melted

FOR THE SYRUP

⅓ cup fresh lemon juice
(from 2 medium lemons)

3 tablespoons fresh
orange juice (from
1 medium orange)

½ cup superfine sugar

FOR THE GLAZE

1 cup confectioners' sugar

2 to 3 tablespoons
fresh lemon juice (from
1 medium lemon)

Candied Lemon Zest
(optional) and Whipped
Cream (page 246), for
serving

1. Make the cake: Preheat oven to 350°F. Spray a 10-cup Bundt pan with oil; dust with flour, tapping out any excess. Finely grate 2 teaspoons lemon zest and ½ teaspoon orange zest. With a sharp knife, remove peel and bitter white pith from all citrus.

2. Holding a lemon over a small bowl, cut between membranes to release segments. Squeeze juice from membranes into another small bowl. Repeat with remaining lemon and orange, combining segments in one bowl and juices in other. Cut segments into ¼-inch pieces. (You will need 3 tablespoons juice and ¾ cup segments.)

3. In a medium bowl, whisk together flour, superfine sugar, baking powder, and salt. With an electric mixer on medium speed, add crème fraîche and beat until combined. Add eggs, one at a time, beating just to combine. Beat in butter, citrus juices, and zests. Add citrus segments and beat just to combine. Transfer batter to prepared pan, smoothing top with a small offset spatula. Bake, rotating pan halfway through, until a cake tester comes out clean, about 48 minutes.

4. Make the syrup: In a small saucepan, bring citrus juices and superfine sugar to a boil, stirring until sugar dissolves. Boil 30 seconds more.

5. Make the glaze: In a small bowl, whisk together confectioners' sugar and lemon juice to taste.

6. To serve: When cake is done, leave oven on and transfer cake to a wire rack set on a baking sheet to cool 15 minutes. Turn out onto rack and cool 10 minutes more. Transfer to a shallow dish. Brush syrup over cake. Continue brushing syrup from dish until all is absorbed. Return cake to wire rack and let dry in oven 5 minutes. Remove from oven and immediately brush with glaze. Let cool completely. (Cake can be stored, covered, up to 1 day.) Top with candied zest, if desired, and serve with whipped cream.

POMEGRANATE-COCONUT TRIFLE

As pretty to look at as they are good for you, pomegranates star in this stunning layered dessert. A deep-crimson pomegranate gelatin on the bottom and a lighter, pomegranate-seed-studded coconut-water one on top enclose a creamy, decadent coconut custard center. **SERVES 8 TO 12**

3 tablespoons unflavored powdered gelatin (from four ¼-ounce envelopes)

1 cup cold water

3 cups 100% pomegranate juice

⅔ cup plus 2 tablespoons superfine sugar

3 tablespoons cornstarch

¼ teaspoon kosher salt

1 cup cream of coconut, such as Coco Lopez

2½ cups cold heavy cream

3 large egg yolks

2 tablespoons unsalted butter

2 teaspoons vanilla extract or paste

16 ladyfingers, halved crosswise

4 cups coconut water, such as Harmless Harvest

¾ cup pomegranate arils (seeds)

1. In a small saucepan, sprinkle gelatin over cold water and let stand 5 minutes. Heat over medium until gelatin dissolves. In a 12- to 14-cup trifle dish or glass bowl, combine pomegranate juice, ⅓ cup sugar, and half of gelatin mixture (reserve remaining gelatin mixture at room temperature), stirring until sugar dissolves. Refrigerate until set, about 4 hours.

2. In a medium saucepan, whisk together cornstarch, salt, cream of coconut, ½ cup heavy cream, and egg yolks until smooth. Add butter and cook over medium heat, stirring occasionally, until mixture comes to a boil. Cook, stirring, until it has the consistency of pudding. Strain through a fine-mesh sieve into a bowl, pressing on solids; discard solids. Stir in vanilla. Cover surface with plastic wrap, pressing it directly onto the surface to prevent a skin from forming, and let cool completely. In a medium bowl, whip 1 cup heavy cream to stiff peaks; fold into cooled coconut custard until smooth.

3. Arrange half of ladyfingers evenly in a single layer over pomegranate gelatin. Spoon coconut custard over top, spreading with an offset spatula until smooth. Top with remaining ladyfingers, in a single layer and refrigerate to chill.

4. Prepare an ice-water bath. In a bowl, stir together coconut water, ⅓ cup sugar, and reserved gelatin mixture until sugar dissolves. Transfer bowl to ice bath; let stand, stirring a few times, until mixture begins to thicken, 20 to 30 minutes. Stir in pomegranate arils. Transfer mixture to trifle dish; smooth top. Refrigerate until set, at least 4 hours or, covered, up to 3 days.

5. In a medium bowl, whisk remaining 1 cup heavy cream and 2 tablespoons sugar to soft peaks. Spoon over trifle and serve.

TIP:
Ladyfingers provide a classic-trifle touch here, dividing the layers. Store-bought ones do the job beautifully.

TIP:
As with any meringue, a sharp, thin-bladed knife is a must for neat slices. Wipe the blade with a warm, damp towel between each cut.

UPSIDE-DOWN LEMON MERINGUE PIE

This delightfully light pie turns the typical lemon-meringue on its head, with the meringue itself taking the place of the usual short-crust pastry. Based on an angel pie that our food editor Laura's grandmother spent years perfecting, it is topped with a cloud of whipped cream and a sprinkling of lemon zest. Chilling time takes most of a day, so plan accordingly. **SERVES 8**

FOR THE CRUST

Unsalted butter, room temperature, for pie dish

4 large egg whites, room temperature

¼ teaspoon cream of tartar

1 cup sugar

FOR THE FILLING

8 large egg yolks, room temperature

1 cup sugar

1 tablespoon plus 1 teaspoon finely grated lemon zest

¼ cup plus 2 tablespoons fresh lemon juice (from 2 lemons)

1 cup cold heavy cream

FOR THE TOPPING

1 cup cold heavy cream

1 tablespoon sugar

Grated zest of 1 lemon, for serving

1. Make the crust: Preheat oven to 300°F with a rack in center. Lightly brush a 9-inch pie dish with butter. With an electric mixer on high speed, whisk together egg whites and 1 tablespoon cold water in a large bowl until foamy, about 30 seconds. Add cream of tartar and continue to beat until soft peaks form, about 1 minute. Gradually add sugar and beat until thick, glossy peaks form, about 5 minutes.

2. Transfer egg-white mixture to prepared pie dish; spread along bottom and up sides to form crust. (Don't spread past rim of dish.) Bake meringue until crisp and light golden on outside, about 40 minutes. Turn off heat and let cool in oven 1 hour, then transfer to a wire rack and let cool completely.

3. Make the filling: In a medium saucepan, off heat, whisk egg yolks until thickened and pale yellow, 1 to 2 minutes. Whisk in sugar and lemon zest and juice. Place over medium heat and cook, stirring constantly with a wooden spoon, until mixture is very thick, about 10 minutes. Transfer to a large bowl. Cover with plastic wrap, pressing it directly onto surface of curd. Refrigerate until thoroughly chilled, at least 1 hour or up to 1 day.

4. Whisk curd until smooth. In a medium bowl, with a mixer on high speed, whip cream until soft peaks form, about 30 seconds. Working in batches, gently fold whipped cream into curd. Fill meringue crust with lightened curd; smooth top. Refrigerate, loosely covered, at least 8 hours or up to 1 day.

5. Make the topping: With a mixer on high speed, whip cream and sugar until stiff peaks form, about 40 seconds. Spread over pie. Sprinkle with lemon zest before serving.

PASSION-FRUIT CHEESECAKE BARS

Add some passion to your winter days. These creamy, layered bars get their speckled golden hue from passion fruit in two ways: Fresh fruit adds texture with its pulp and seeds, while frozen purée, a common baking ingredient found in major supermarkets, heightens the flavor. **SERVES 8**

FOR THE CRUST

4 tablespoons unsalted butter, melted, plus more for pan

6 graham cracker sheets

3 ounces pecans, toasted (page 246) and chopped (¾ cup)

¼ cup sugar

FOR THE FILLING

2 packages (8 ounces each) cream cheese, room temperature

¾ cup sugar

¼ cup sour cream

¼ cup passion-fruit purée, such as Les Vergers Boiron, thawed if frozen

1 teaspoon vanilla extract

2 large eggs

FOR THE TOPPING

1 envelope (¼ ounce) unflavored powdered gelatin

½ cup cold water

1 cup passion-fruit purée, thawed if frozen

¼ cup sugar

½ cup passion-fruit pulp (from 4 fresh passion fruits)

1. Make the crust: Preheat oven to 325°F. Lightly butter an 8-inch square baking pan. Line with parchment, leaving a 2-inch overhang on two sides; butter parchment. Pulse graham cracker until finely ground in a food processor (you should have ¾ cup). Add pecans and continue to pulse until finely chopped. Add sugar and butter, and pulse to combine. Using a rubber spatula, transfer graham cracker mixture to prepared pan, pressing firmly into bottom of pan. Bake crust until light golden, about 12 minutes. Transfer to a wire rack to cool. (Don't turn off oven.)

2. Make the filling: With an electric mixer on medium speed, beat cream cheese and sugar in a medium bowl until light and fluffy, about 3 minutes. Add sour cream, passion-fruit purée, and vanilla, and beat until combined. Add eggs, one at a time, beating well after each addition. Pour filling over baked crust, smoothing top with a small offset spatula. Bake until puffed and set along edges but still slightly wobbly in center, 40 to 45 minutes. Transfer to a wire rack to cool completely at room temperature.

3. Make the topping: In a small bowl, sprinkle gelatin over cold water. Let stand 5 minutes. Meanwhile, in a small saucepan, bring passion-fruit purée and sugar to a boil. Immediately remove from heat and whisk in gelatin mixture until sugar dissolves. Let cool to room temperature, about 45 minutes. Stir fresh passion-fruit pulp and seeds into gelatin mixture. Pour on top of cooled cheesecake. Refrigerate until chilled, at least 4 hours or, covered, up to 3 days. Slice into bars with a sharp knife, wiping the blade between cuts, and serve.

TROPICAL-FRUIT CONES

Brighten up a dreary winter day with a vivid rainbow of sorbet-like frozen fruit purées. Use mango, banana, or kiwi—or all three. The riper the fruit, the creamier and more color-saturated they become. For serving, dip old-fashioned sugar cones in chocolate and coat them with natural sprinkles, nuts, or nonpareils. **MAKES 2 CUPS (SERVES 8 SINGLE SCOOPS)**

2 very ripe large mangoes, 4 very ripe bananas, or 8 very ripe kiwis, peeled, cut into ¾-inch pieces, and frozen on a parchment-lined baking sheet

Pinch of kosher salt

6 ounces high-quality white chocolate, such as Valrhona, chopped

8 sugar cones

Chocolate and natural sprinkles, nonpareils, and finely chopped nuts, such as pistachios, for decorating

1. Pulse frozen fruit and salt in a food processor until smooth. Transfer to a freezer-safe container, cover surface with plastic wrap, and freeze until firm, at least 2 hours or up to 1 week.

2. Melt chocolate in a heatproof bowl set over (not in) a pot of simmering water; set aside to cool slightly. Dip tops of cones in melted chocolate and sprinkle with candies, nuts, or a combination. Freeze until set, at least 5 minutes or up to 1 day.

3. To serve, refrigerate purées until slightly softened, about 15 minutes. Scoop into cones and serve immediately.

TIP:
You can use any tropical fruit you like for these treats. If you have a sweet tooth, add 2 tablespoons agave nectar to the frozen mango or kiwi. If you prefer a little tang, add 2 tablespoons fresh lime juice to the mango.

MEYER LEMON SOUFFLÉS

These lofty citrus soufflés offer a burst of sunshine in the middle of winter.
Serve these delicate individual portions straight from the oven,
dusted with confectioners' sugar and with a side of crème fraîche. **MAKES 6**

Unsalted butter,
room temperature,
for ramekins

¼ cup plus 2 tablespoons
superfine sugar,
plus more for ramekins

1 cup whole milk

1 vanilla bean,
split and seeds scraped,
pod reserved

Pinch of kosher salt

3 large egg yolks
plus 5 large egg whites,
room temperature

¼ cup unbleached
all-purpose flour

2 teaspoons finely
grated Meyer lemon zest
plus ¼ cup fresh juice

Pinch of cream of tartar

Confectioners' sugar,
for dusting

Crème fraîche, for serving

1. Preheat oven to 400°F with a rack in lower third. Butter six 6-ounce ramekins and coat with superfine sugar (to help the soufflé climb up the sides as it bakes). Place on a rimmed baking sheet.

2. In a medium saucepan, bring milk, vanilla pod and seeds, and salt to a simmer over medium-low heat. In a large bowl, whisk together yolks and ¼ cup superfine sugar until pale and fluffy, 1 to 2 minutes. Add flour and whisk until well combined.

3. Remove vanilla pod from milk mixture (discard or reserve for another use), then gradually add half of milk mixture to yolk mixture, whisking constantly. Whisk yolk mixture into remaining milk mixture in saucepan and bring just to a boil, whisking constantly. Reduce heat and simmer until thick and smooth, 1 to 2 minutes. Remove from heat and whisk in lemon zest and juice. Transfer to a large bowl and cover with plastic wrap, pressing it directly onto surface of mixture. Let cool completely.

4. In another large bowl, whisk egg whites and cream of tartar until soft peaks form. Gradually add remaining 2 tablespoons superfine sugar and whisk until peaks are stiff and glossy, about 2 minutes.

5. Spoon one-quarter of whites mixture into custard base, then whisk thoroughly until smooth. Using a large flexible spatula, gently fold in remaining whites mixture until just combined (don't overmix). Divide evenly among prepared ramekins. Bake until risen and set, about 15 minutes. (They deflate quickly once removed from the oven.) Dust with confectioners' sugar and serve immediately with crème fraîche.

TROPICAL FRUIT CREPE CAKE

Technically speaking, this isn't a cake at all—it's a towering stack of paper-thin pancakes, layered with luscious, coconut-infused pastry cream. You can and should assemble this ahead, allowing plenty of time for it to chill and set before topping with more tropical fruit. **SERVES 8**

FOR THE PASTRY CREAM

6⅔ cups whole milk

1½ cups flaked coconut, toasted (page 246)

½ teaspoon kosher salt

1⅓ cups granulated sugar

⅔ cup cornstarch

10 large egg yolks

6 tablespoons unsalted butter, room temperature

1 cup cold heavy cream

FOR THE CREPES

1½ cups unbleached all-purpose flour

1 cup granulated sugar

½ teaspoon kosher salt

2½ cups whole milk, room temperature

6 large eggs, room temperature

2 teaspoons vanilla extract

1½ sticks (¾ cup) unsalted butter, melted, plus more for pan

1 cup cold heavy cream

2 tablespoons confectioners' sugar

Sliced pineapple and toasted coconut (page 246), for topping

1. Make the pastry cream: In a large saucepan, bring milk, coconut, and salt to just under a boil. Remove from heat, cover, and let stand until cool, about 2 hours. Strain through a fine-mesh sieve; discard solids. In a medium saucepan, off heat, whisk together sugar and cornstarch. Whisk in egg yolks, then cooled milk mixture. Stir in butter. Bring to a boil over medium heat and continue to cook 1 minute, whisking constantly. Pass through a fine-mesh sieve. Cover with plastic wrap, pressing it directly onto surface of pastry cream to prevent a skin from forming. Refrigerate until chilled, at least 2 hours and up to 2 days.

2. Make the crepes: Combine flour, sugar, salt, milk, eggs, vanilla, and melted butter in a blender. Blend until smooth. Refrigerate for at least 1 hour and up to overnight.

3. Lightly brush an 8-inch nonstick skillet or crepe pan with butter. Heat over medium until just starting to smoke. Remove from heat and pour a scant 2 tablespoons batter into center of pan, swirling to cover bottom. Cook until edges are golden and center is dry, about 30 seconds. Flip and cook about 20 seconds more. Slide crepe onto a parchment-lined baking sheet. Repeat with remaining batter, brushing skillet with more butter and adjusting heat as needed; stack crepes as you go (you should end up with about 40). Let cool completely.

4. Whisk chilled pastry cream to remove any lumps. In a medium bowl, whip heavy cream to stiff peaks. Fold into pastry cream. Place one crepe on a flat serving dish. Spread about ¼ cup pastry cream onto crepe. Repeat process with remaining crepes and pastry cream, finishing with a crepe. Refrigerate until set, at least 2 hours and up to overnight.

5. To serve, whip heavy cream with confectioners' sugar to stiff peaks. Arrange pineapple slices on top of cake, overlapping slightly. Dollop whipped cream on top. Garnish with toasted coconut.

WHOLE-LEMON POUND CAKE WITH POMEGRANATE GLAZE

Move over, lemon zest: This cake gets a whole lemon—boiled, chopped, then stirred, pith and all, into the batter. It's somehow more intensely lemony yet less sharp than zest and juice alone. A pomegranate joins the fun—the juice tints the glaze pink, while the seeds are scattered across the top. **SERVES 10**

1 lemon

2 sticks (1 cup) unsalted butter, room temperature, plus more for pan

1²/₃ cups unbleached all-purpose flour, plus more for pan

1½ teaspoons baking powder

1 teaspoon kosher salt

1¼ cups granulated sugar

4 large eggs, room temperature

1 teaspoon vanilla extract

FOR THE GLAZE

¾ cup confectioners' sugar, sifted

2 to 4 teaspoons 100% pomegranate juice

2 teaspoons whole milk (optional)

⅓ cup pomegranate arils (seeds)

1. In a medium saucepan, cover whole lemon by at least 3 inches of water. Place over medium-high heat and bring to a boil. Continue to boil until lemon is tender, about 30 minutes; drain, pat dry, and let cool. When cool enough to handle, roughly chop lemon, removing any visible seeds. Pulse in a food processor until finely chopped.

2. Preheat oven to 325°F. Butter a 4½-by-8½-inch loaf pan; dust with flour, tapping out any excess. In a medium bowl, whisk together flour, baking powder, and salt.

3. With an electric mixer on medium-high speed, beat butter and granulated sugar until pale and fluffy, about 4 minutes, scraping down sides of bowl as needed. Add eggs, one at a time, beating thoroughly after each and scraping down sides of bowl as needed. Mix in vanilla. Reduce speed to low; add flour mixture in two batches, alternating with chopped lemon and beginning and ending with flour mixture, beating until just incorporated.

4. Transfer batter to prepared pan, smoothing top with an offset spatula. Bake until a cake tester comes out clean, about 1 hour 25 minutes. Transfer pan to a wire rack to cool 30 minutes. Turn out cake onto rack to cool completely.

5. Make the glaze: In a medium bowl, whisk together confectioners' sugar and 2 teaspoons pomegranate juice. Add up to 2 more teaspoons pomegranate juice, ½ teaspoon at a time, until glaze is thick yet pourable. (For a lighter pink glaze, substitute with 2 teaspoons whole milk.) Pour pomegranate glaze over cooled cake. Top with pomegranate arils. Let set, at least 30 minutes, before slicing to serve.

TANGERINE CHIFFON TART

A chiffon filling is both light and sumptuous; it gets its structure from eggs and gelatin, and in this case, its intensely citrusy flavor from sweet tangerine juice. Finished with edible blooms, this tart is almost too pretty to eat. **SERVES 8**

FOR THE CRUST

12 graham crackers sheets

3 tablespoons sugar

5 tablespoons unsalted butter, melted

FOR THE FILLING

1 teaspoon finely grated tangerine zest plus 2 cups freshly squeezed juice (from about 12 tangerines)

2 tablespoons fresh lemon juice (from 1 lemon)

2 tablespoons cold water

2 teaspoons unflavored gelatin (from one ¼-ounce envelope)

5 large eggs, separated, room temperature

¾ cup sugar

¼ teaspoon kosher salt

Pinch of cream of tartar

Unsprayed fresh edible flowers, such as micro marigolds, for serving (optional; available at gourmetsweet botanicals.com)

1. Make the crust: Preheat oven to 350°F. Pulse graham crackers and sugar in a food processor until finely ground. Add butter and pulse until mixture has texture of wet sand. Press into bottom and up sides of a 9-inch tart pan with a removable bottom. Place pan on a baking sheet, and bake until crust is fragrant and slightly colored, about 12 minutes. Transfer pan to a wire rack to cool.

2. Make the filling: In a small saucepan, bring tangerine juice to a boil. Continue to cook until juice has reduced to 1 cup, about 18 minutes.

3. In a small bowl, combine lemon juice and cold water. Sprinkle with gelatin and let stand 5 minutes. In a medium saucepan, whisk together egg yolks, ½ cup sugar, the reduced tangerine juice, tangerine zest, and salt. Bring to a boil, then reduce heat to medium and simmer, stirring constantly, until thickened, about 10 minutes. Strain mixture through a fine-mesh sieve into a medium heatproof bowl; discard solids. Add gelatin mixture to tangerine curd, whisking until gelatin is dissolved. Refrigerate, stirring frequently, until thickened slightly but not fully set, 20 to 30 minutes, being careful not to overchill.

4. Beat egg whites and cream of tartar in the bowl of an electric mixer fitted with the whisk attachment on medium-high speed until foamy, about 2 minutes. Gradually add remaining ¼ cup sugar and continue to beat on medium-high until firm peaks form, 3 to 5 minutes more. Gently fold beaten egg whites into chilled tangerine mixture in 3 batches. Mound into cooled crust. Refrigerate until set, at least 2 hours or up to overnight. Sprinkle with flowers, if desired, and serve.

SPRING

The thaw brings early signs of life—and sweet, precocious produce to the table. A few standout stars bridge the gap between winter's tropical respite and summer's ripe bounty. Enjoy them while you can in cobblers, tarts, crumbles, and more.

GIANT STRAWBERRY "SHORTCAKE"

Move over, shortcake, the grown-ups are having a party. This sparkling, sugar-coated tart shell overflowing with cream and berries strikes a more refined note than its rustic inspiration—as does a drizzle of subtly floral elderflower liqueur. Scatter a few additional berries or fresh elderflowers over the tart before serving. **SERVES 10 TO 12**

FOR THE TART SHELL

1¼ cups unbleached all-purpose flour, plus more for dusting

½ teaspoon kosher salt

1 stick (½ cup) cold unsalted butter, cut into pieces

2 to 4 tablespoons ice-cold water

1 large egg, separated

3 tablespoons coarse sanding sugar, for sprinkling

FOR THE STRAWBERRY TOPPING

1½ pounds strawberries, hulled and sliced, plus more (optional) halved berries for serving

¼ cup granulated sugar

1 tablespoon elderflower liqueur

1 teaspoon fresh lemon juice

FOR THE WHIPPED CREAM

1 cup cold heavy cream

½ cup confectioners' sugar

1. Make the tart shell: Pulse flour and salt in a food processor until combined. Add butter and pulse until mixture resembles coarse meal, with a few pea-size pieces of butter remaining. Drizzle in 2 tablespoons ice water, then slowly add egg yolk, pulsing until dough just holds together. If dough is too dry, add up to 2 tablespoons more ice water, 1 tablespoon at a time, and pulse. Don't overmix. Shape dough into a disk and wrap in plastic. Refrigerate until firm, at least 1 hour or up 3 days.

2. On a lightly floured piece of parchment, roll dough into a 10-inch circle. Press top of a 9-inch tart pan into dough to stamp out a fluted circle. Transfer parchment with dough onto a baking sheet and freeze until firm, at least 30 minutes.

3. Preheat oven to 325°F. In a small bowl, whisk egg white with a splash of water. Remove dough from freezer and brush top with egg wash. Sprinkle evenly with sanding sugar. Bake until crust is golden and cooked through, 30 to 35 minutes. Transfer to a wire rack to cool, about 20 minutes.

4. Make the strawberry topping: While tart shell cools, toss strawberries with granulated sugar, elderflower liqueur, and lemon juice in a medium bowl; let sit 10 minutes until strawberries release some of their juices.

5. Make the whipped cream: In a chilled large bowl and using an electric mixer on medium-high speed, whisk heavy cream until soft peaks form, about 3 minutes. Add confectioners' sugar and whisk until medium-stiff peaks form, about 2 minutes more. Dollop whipped cream over cooled tart shell. Spoon berries and any juices over top. Top with more berries, if desired, and serve.

MANGO–COCONUT CREAM TART

We used Champagne mangoes for this—if you haven't tried them, they are a must for their creamy texture and honey notes. Blind-baking the pâte brisée before filling ensures a crisp, flaky crust and an even surface to fill with coconut cream and whorls of thinly sliced fruit. **SERVES 10**

1 disk Pâte Brisée
(page 236)

Unbleached all-purpose
flour, for dusting

FOR THE FILLING

²⁄₃ cup granulated sugar

¹⁄₃ cup packed
light-brown sugar

¹⁄₂ teaspoon kosher salt

2 teaspoons fine cornmeal

2 large whole eggs
plus 1 large egg yolk

¹⁄₂ teaspoon
vanilla extract

6 tablespoons unsalted
butter, melted

1¹⁄₄ cups unsweetened
small coconut flakes,
such as Bob's Red Mill,
toasted (page 246)

FOR THE TOPPING

2 firm, ripe mangoes,
preferably Champagne
(1¹⁄₄ pounds total)

Juice of ¹⁄₂ lemon

1¹⁄₂ cups cold
heavy cream

¹⁄₄ cup
confectioners' sugar

1 tablespoon
light corn syrup

1. Preheat oven to 375°F. Roll out pâte brisée to a 15-inch round, about ¹⁄₈ inch thick, on a lightly floured surface. Fit dough into a 12¹⁄₂-inch fluted tart pan with a removable bottom, pressing dough into pan's edge and up sides. Trim edge flush with top rim of pan. Pierce bottom all over with a fork. Freeze until hard, about 20 minutes. Line with parchment, pressing parchment deep into corners of pan so it is flush with dough and leaving a 3-inch over-hang. Fold overhang over dough edge so it is not exposed. Fill with pie weights or dried beans and bake until edge of shell begins to turn golden, about 30 minutes, rotating halfway through. Remove weights and parchment. Reduce oven temperature to 325°F. Tent edge with foil and bake until golden brown, 25 to 27 minutes more. Let cool slightly, about 20 minutes.

2. Make the filling: In a medium bowl, mix together granulated and brown sugars, salt, and cornmeal. Whisk in eggs, yolk, and vanilla, then butter and coconut. Spread filling into tart shell, smoothing top with a small offset spatula. Bake until just set and lightly golden, 22 to 24 minutes. Let cool completely.

3. Make the topping: Peel mangoes and cut each half off the pit. Brush with lemon juice. Very thinly slice each half crosswise. With an electric mixer, beat together cream and confectioners' sugar in a medium bowl until medium peaks form. Spread one-third of cream mixture over top of filling. Fill a pastry bag fitted with a large open star tip (such as Ateco #829) with remain-ing cream mixture and pipe randomly spaced swirls of cream. Twist 3 to 5 mango slices at a time into spirals and nestle them between cream swirls. In a small saucepan over medium-low, heat corn syrup and 2 teaspoons water until combined. Brush mango spirals with syrup. Refrigerate tart until chilled, at least 20 minutes or up to 4 hours. Remove outer ring of pan and serve.

STRAWBERRY-RHUBARB TART

These sweet-tart mainstays of the spring garden just make delicious sense together. To give the classic pie a chic update and really showcase its ruby-red filling, we skipped the double crust and baked it in a springform pan instead. **SERVES 8**

FOR THE CRUST

1 large egg yolk

2 to 4 tablespoons ice-cold water

1¼ cups unbleached all-purpose flour, plus more for dusting

2 tablespoons sugar

1 teaspoon kosher salt

1 stick (½ cup) cold unsalted butter, cut into pieces

Vegetable oil cooking spray

FOR THE FILLING

12 ounces rhubarb, cut on the diagonal into 1-inch pieces (3 cups)

8 ounces strawberries, hulled and cut into ½-inch pieces (1¼ cups)

¾ cup sugar

1 tablespoon plus 2 teaspoons cornstarch

¾ teaspoon kosher salt

1 tablespoon fresh lemon juice

1. Make the crust: In a small bowl, lightly beat egg yolk and 2 tablespoons ice water until combined. Pulse flour, sugar, and salt in a food processor to combine. Add butter and process until mixture resembles coarse meal, with some pea-size pieces of butter remaining, about 10 seconds. With machine running, add yolk mixture in a slow, steady stream. Pulse just until mixture holds together. If dough is too dry, add up to 2 tablespoons ice water, 1 tablespoon at a time. Shape dough into a disk and wrap in plastic. Refrigerate until firm, at least 30 minutes or up to overnight.

2. Preheat oven to 375°F with racks in center and bottom. Spray bottom and sides of a 9-inch springform pan with oil. Let dough stand until pliable. On a lightly floured surface, roll out dough slightly thicker than ⅛ inch. Cut out an 11-inch round. Fit into bottom and up sides of prepared pan. Freeze 15 minutes.

3. Make the filling: In a large bowl, stir together rhubarb, strawberries, sugar, cornstarch, salt, and lemon juice. Pour into tart shell, smoothing top with a small offset spatula. Bake on center rack, with a foil-lined rimmed baking sheet on bottom rack to catch juices, until bubbling in center, about 1 hour 15 minutes. (If crust is browning too quickly, tent with foil during last 15 minutes.) Remove from oven. Release sides of pan immediately. Transfer tart, on pan base, to a wire rack to cool. Serve warm or at room temperature.

STRAWBERRY-LEMONADE ICEBOX CAKE

Jam made with in-season strawberries is one of spring's great joys. Layer it with tart lemon curd and whipped cream for cool, no-bake satisfaction. Freeze well, then add a meringue topping when you're ready to serve. **SERVES 10**

FOR THE STRAWBERRY JAM

1 pound strawberries, hulled and cut into $\frac{1}{2}$-inch pieces (about 3 cups)

$\frac{1}{2}$ cup sugar

1 tablespoon fresh lemon juice

FOR THE FILLING

$\frac{1}{2}$ cup sugar

4 large egg yolks (reserve 2 egg whites for meringue, remaining 2 for another use)

1 tablespoon finely grated lemon zest plus $\frac{2}{3}$ cup fresh lemon juice (from 4 lemons)

$\frac{1}{4}$ teaspoon kosher salt

5 tablespoons unsalted butter, cut into $\frac{1}{2}$-inch pieces

2 cups cold heavy cream

Vegetable oil cooking spray

11 graham cracker sheets, broken into pieces

FOR THE TOPPING

2 large egg whites, room temperature (reserved from filling)

$\frac{1}{3}$ cup sugar

1. Make the jam: In a small saucepan, heat strawberries, sugar, and lemon juice over medium. Cook until bubbling, thickened, and fruit has broken down, 15 to 20 minutes. Transfer to a heatproof bowl and refrigerate until cool (you should have about 1¼ cups jam).

2. Make the filling: In a small saucepan, off heat, whisk together sugar and egg yolks; whisk in lemon zest and juice and salt. Add butter and cook over medium heat, whisking constantly, until butter melts and mixture is thick enough to coat the back of a spoon, about 3 minutes. Pour curd through a fine-mesh sieve into a heatproof bowl. Press plastic wrap against surface and refrigerate until cool. In a large bowl, whip cream until medium peaks form. With a rubber spatula, gently fold cooled lemon curd into whipped cream.

3. Assemble the cake: Spray a 9-by-5-inch loaf pan with oil. Line with 2 sheets of plastic wrap, leaving a 3-inch overhang on long sides. Spray plastic wrap with oil. Using a small offset spatula, spread a third of the lemonade filling in prepared pan. Dollop half the cooled strawberry jam over lemonade filling. Arrange a single layer of graham crackers. Repeat layering process with another third of lemonade filling, remaining jam, and a layer of graham crackers. Spread remaining third of lemonade filling over graham crackers. Wrap with overhanging plastic and freeze at least 8 hours or up to 2 weeks.

4. Make the topping: In a heatproof bowl set over (not in) a pan of simmering water, heat egg whites and sugar, whisking constantly, until mixture is warm to the touch and no longer feels grainy when rubbed between two fingers. Remove from heat. With an electric mixer on high speed, whisk until medium peaks form, 6 to 8 minutes. Invert cake onto a serving platter and remove plastic. Spoon meringue over top. Use a kitchen torch to lightly brown meringue, moving flame back and forth until evenly browned. Use a sharp knife to cut, wiping between slices, and serve.

STRAWBERRY JAM COBBLER

It doesn't get better than homemade strawberry jam on a freshly baked biscuit, unless you flip the two and bake the biscuit dough atop a pool of jam to create a warm, bubbling cobbler. This is a dreamy way to celebrate the bounty you bring home from a day of strawberry picking. Serve with whipped cream or a scoop of vanilla ice cream. **SERVES 8**

FOR THE JAM

2 pounds strawberries, hulled and sliced into ½-inch pieces (about 5½ cups)

2 cups granulated sugar

1 tablespoon fresh lemon juice

FOR THE BISCUITS

1¾ cups unbleached all-purpose flour

1¾ teaspoons baking powder

¼ cup granulated sugar

¾ teaspoon kosher salt

6 tablespoons cold unsalted butter, cut into pieces

¾ cup cold heavy cream, plus more for brushing

Coarse sanding sugar, for sprinkling

Whipped Cream (page 246), for serving

1. Make the jam: In a large pot over medium-high heat, cook strawberries, granulated sugar, and lemon juice, stirring occasionally, until fruit breaks down slightly and is reduced to 4 cups, about 12 minutes. Let cool completely. (Jam can be stored in refrigerator for up to 3 days.)

2. Make the biscuits: Preheat oven to 375°F with a rack in lower third and a foil-lined baking sheet on rack below. In a medium bowl, whisk together flour, baking powder, granulated sugar, and salt. Cut in butter with a pastry blender, or rub in with your fingers, until mixture resembles coarse meal with some large pea-size pieces remaining. With a fork, mix in cream until dough starts to come together but is still crumbly. Turn out onto a lightly floured work surface; knead once or twice to make smooth. Pat dough into an 8-inch round, about ¾ inch thick. Cut into 8 wedges.

3. Spread 3 cups jam in bottom of a 9½-inch deep-dish pie plate or skillet. Arrange dough on top, wedges fitted together in original round shape; then brush with heavy cream and sprinkle with sanding sugar. Bake until bubbling and golden (if top is browning too quickly, tent with foil), about 50 minutes. Transfer to a wire rack to cool. Serve with remaining jam and whipped cream.

STRAWBERRY-BANANA PUDDING

Just about every Southerner has a go-to banana pudding recipe that includes vanilla wafers, ripe bananas, and rich custard. This dessert does that classic one better, giving it a bright boost of just-picked strawberries. The cooked pudding takes several hours to fully set up, so start the day before. **SERVES 12**

1 cup granulated sugar

¼ cup plus
2 tablespoons
cornstarch

½ teaspoon kosher salt

½ vanilla bean,
split and seeds scraped,
pod reserved

5 cups whole milk

8 large egg yolks

4 tablespoons unsalted
butter, cut into pieces

2½ cups
cold heavy cream

2 tablespoons
confectioners' sugar

72 wafer-style
vanilla cookies, such
as Nilla Wafers (from
one 11-ounce box)

4 large bananas,
cut crosswise
into ¼-inch slices

1 pound strawberries,
hulled and cut into
¼-inch slices

1. In a medium saucepan, off heat, whisk together granulated sugar, cornstarch, salt, and vanilla seeds and pod. Gradually whisk in milk until cornstarch is dissolved; whisk in egg yolks.

2. Cook over medium, whisking constantly, until the first large bubble forms and sputters. Reduce heat to low; cook, whisking constantly, 1 minute. Remove from heat and stir in butter until melted. Immediately pour through a fine-mesh sieve into a medium bowl; remove vanilla pod. Cover with plastic wrap, pressing directly onto surface to prevent skin from forming. Let cool completely.

3. In a medium bowl, whisk cream and confectioners' sugar until stiff peaks form. Spoon one-third of pudding into a large glass bowl. Layer half of cookies, slightly overlapping, followed by half of bananas and half of strawberries. Spread one-third of whipped cream over fruit. Repeat layering of pudding, cookies, fruit, and whipped cream. Gently spread with remaining pudding; top with remaining whipped cream. Refrigerate until set, at least 4 hours or, covered, up to overnight.

STRAWBERRY-SWIRL BUNDT

This stunner uses strawberries two ways: fresh macerated ones for a luscious filling and ground freeze-dried ones for the sweet pink cake-batter swirl. The berry powder provides flavor without weighing down the cake's tender crumb. **SERVES 12 TO 16**

3 sticks (1½ cups) unsalted butter, room temperature, plus more for pan

3½ cups cake flour (not self-rising), whisked, plus more for pan

5 to 6 large egg whites (⅔ cup), room temperature

¾ cup whole milk

2½ teaspoons vanilla extract

1¾ cups plus 3 tablespoons granulated sugar

Kosher salt

4 teaspoons baking powder

4 tablespoons ground freeze-dried strawberries (½ ounce)

2 drops pink gel-paste food coloring

1 pint fresh strawberries, hulled and sliced (2½ cups)

1 cup cold heavy cream

2 tablespoons confectioners' sugar, plus more for dusting

1. Preheat oven to 350°F with a rack in center. Butter a 10- to 15-cup Bundt pan; dust with flour, tapping out excess. In a medium bowl, whisk together egg whites, milk, and vanilla until combined. In a large bowl, beat butter, 1¾ cups granulated sugar, 1¾ teaspoons salt, and the baking powder with an electric mixer on medium-high speed until light and fluffy, 2 to 3 minutes. Reduce speed to low and add flour in three batches, alternating with egg-white mixture and beginning and ending with flour. Separate 2 cups batter and stir in freeze-dried strawberries.

2. Transfer ¼ cup strawberry batter to a small bowl; stir in pink gel paste, a little at a time, until desired color is achieved. Stir mixture back into remaining strawberry batter until combined.

3. Spoon 2½ cups vanilla batter into bottom of prepared pan. Top with all the strawberry batter, then remaining vanilla batter. Run a butter knife through batter four times to swirl, then use butter knife to fold and swoop in a couple places to further marble.

4. Transfer pan to oven and reduce temperature to 325°F. Bake until top of cake springs back when lightly touched and a cake tester comes out clean, about 1 hour. Transfer pan to a wire rack to cool 15 minutes. Turn out cake onto rack and let cool completely.

5. In a medium bowl, stir together fresh strawberries, remaining 3 tablespoons granulated sugar, and a pinch of salt; let stand until sugar dissolves, about 15 minutes. Meanwhile, with mixer on high speed, beat cream with confectioners' sugar to soft peaks. Dust cake with more confectioners' sugar and serve topped with whipped cream and macerated berries.

VANILLA RHUBARB TART

Though classified as a vegetable, rhubarb, with its rosy, celery-like stalks, is at its best in sweet jams and desserts. Here its slightly tart flavor pairs beautifully with warm vanilla bean–infused sugar. For an impress-your-guests presentation, trim pieces diagonally and alternate rows, herringbone-style—or give it your own angle. **SERVES 8**

1 disk Pâte Brisée
(page 236)

Unbleached all-purpose
flour, for dusting

1 cup granulated sugar

1 tablespoon cornstarch

¾ teaspoon kosher salt

1 vanilla bean, split
and seeds scraped

1 pound rhubarb
(about 6 stalks), halved
lengthwise, then
cut on the bias into
1¼-inch pieces

2 teaspoons fresh
lemon juice

1 large egg, lightly
beaten, for egg wash

Coarse sanding sugar,
for sprinkling

1. Preheat oven to 375°F. Line a baking sheet with parchment. Roll out pâte brisée to a 10-by-13-inch rectangle, about ⅛ inch thick, on a lightly floured surface. Transfer to prepared sheet and refrigerate 15 minutes.

2. In a medium bowl, whisk together granulated sugar, cornstarch, and salt. Using your fingers, work vanilla seeds through mixture evenly. Add rhubarb and lemon juice, and stir to combine.

3. Arrange rhubarb mixture over dough, in a herringbone pattern as shown, if desired, leaving a 1-inch border. Fold edges of dough over to partially cover rhubarb. Brush crust with egg wash and sprinkle with sanding sugar.

4. Bake until bubbling in center, 45 to 50 minutes. Using a pastry brush, spread bubbling juices over rhubarb to glaze. Let cool at least 30 minutes. Tart can be stored, tented with parchment-lined foil, at room temperature up to 1 day.

MANGO KULFI

Kulfi, an Indian frozen dessert similar to ice cream, traditionally starts with milk being simmered for hours. Once caramelized, it's frozen in aluminum molds. For this creamy homemade version, we cut that cooking time down by adding milk powder and condensed milk. **SERVES 8 TO 10**

2 very ripe medium mangoes (about 2 pounds), pitted, peeled, and chopped (about 1½ cups)

2 cups whole milk

¼ cup nonfat milk powder

1 can (14 ounces) sweetened condensed milk

¼ teaspoon freshly ground cardamom (see Tip)

¼ teaspoon kosher salt

2 tablespoons roughly chopped pistachios, for garnish

1. In a blender, purée mangoes; reserve 1 cup (save remaining for another use).

2. In a wide nonstick saucepan, bring milk to a boil over medium-high heat. Reduce to medium-low and continue to cook until reduced by half, about 20 minutes, stirring frequently to avoid scorching milk. Whisk in milk powder, condensed milk, cardamom, and salt. Let cool for 15 minutes. Whisk in reserved mango purée.

3. Divide mixture among 8 to 10 individual freezer-safe cups or molds, filling 3 to 4 ounces each. Insert a wooden stick, cover with plastic wrap, and freeze until solid, at least 6 hours or up to 1 week. Remove pops from molds and sprinkle with chopped pistachios just before serving.

TIP:
Sweet and somewhat spicy, cardamom seeds come in green, black, and white and are available as pods, seeds, or ground into a powder. To freshly grind seeds, squeeze them from the pod (if necessary) and grind them with a mortar and pestle until fine. Alternately, seal them in a plastic bag and crush them into a fine powder with a rolling pin.

LEMON-RHUBARB BUNDT

Here's a zingy (and dairy-free!) twist on the standard lemon Bundt: Olive oil and whipped egg whites yield a light, fluffy texture, and each citrusy slice is flecked with rhubarb. The trick behind the sparkling shell? Coat the pan with sanding sugar instead of flour. **SERVES 10 TO 12**

1¼ cups extra-virgin olive oil, plus more for pan

Coarse sanding sugar, for pan

2 cups unbleached all-purpose flour

½ cup fine yellow cornmeal

1 teaspoon baking powder

½ teaspoon baking soda

1¼ teaspoons kosher salt

3 large eggs, separated, room temperature

1¼ cups plus 2 tablespoons granulated sugar

2 teaspoons vanilla extract or paste

2 teaspoons grated lemon zest plus ¼ cup fresh juice (from 1 to 2 lemons)

8 ounces rhubarb, cut into ½-inch dice (2 cups)

1. Preheat oven to 350°F. Brush a 10- to 15-cup Bundt pan with oil; generously sprinkle with sanding sugar to fully coat (do not tap out excess).

2. In a large bowl, whisk together flour, cornmeal, baking powder, baking soda, and salt. In another large bowl, whisk together oil, egg yolks, 1 cup granulated sugar, the vanilla, and lemon zest and juice.

3. In a large bowl, with an electric mixer on low speed, beat egg whites until foamy. Increase speed to medium-high and gradually add ¼ cup granulated sugar, beating until stiff, glossy peaks form. Stir oil mixture into flour mixture just to combine. Stir one-third of egg-white mixture into batter, then gently fold in remaining egg-white mixture just until no streaks remain (do not overmix).

4. In a small bowl, toss rhubarb with remaining 2 tablespoons granulated sugar to evenly coat. Fold rhubarb mixture into batter, then transfer to prepared pan, smoothing top with a small offset spatula. Bake until cake is golden brown on top and a cake tester comes out clean, 45 to 50 minutes (if top is browning too quickly, tent with foil). Transfer to a wire rack to cool, about 15 minutes. Turn out on rack and cool completely before serving.

MANGO–KEY LIME TART

Puréed ripe mango adds a tropical note to sublime dessert. We used the juice and zest of tiny Key limes for their beloved fragrance and pleasing acidity, but regular Persian limes or even lemons will do in a pinch. **SERVES 10**

10 graham cracker sheets, broken into pieces

2 tablespoons sugar

5 tablespoons unsalted butter, melted

3 cups diced mango (from 2 to 3 pitted, peeled large mangoes), plus more for serving

1 can (14 ounces) sweetened condensed milk

½ teaspoon finely grated Key lime zest plus 3 tablespoons juice (from about 4 Key limes)

4 large egg yolks

¼ teaspoon kosher salt

Whipped Cream (page 246), for serving

1. Preheat oven to 350°F. Pulse graham crackers and sugar in a food processor until finely ground (you should have about 1¼ cups). Add butter and pulse just until combined. Transfer mixture to a 9-inch tart pan with a removable bottom; press into bottom and up sides. Place pan on a baking sheet and bake until crust is fragrant and slightly darker, 10 to 12 minutes. Transfer to a wire rack to cool completely.

2. Purée mangoes in food processor. Strain through a fine-mesh sieve, pressing to extract purée; discard solids. In a bowl, whisk together 1¼ cups strained mango purée, condensed milk, lime zest and juice, yolks, and salt. Pour into crust. Bake until filling is set around edges but still slightly loose in center, about 25 minutes.

3. Transfer tart to a wire rack to cool 1 hour, then refrigerate until chilled, at least 2 hours or up to overnight. Serve with whipped cream and diced mango on the side.

STRAWBERRY AND APRICOT CRISP WITH PINE-NUT CRUMBLE

This easy fruit crisp has all the juicy, buttery goodness of a summer tart, with no fussy crust. The strawberries cook down to a saucy texture, enveloping the apricot slices, which hold their shape. It's delicious at room temperature but even better warm, maybe with a scoop of strawberry ice cream. **SERVES 6**

FOR THE TOPPING

½ cup packed
light-brown sugar

⅓ cup unbleached
all-purpose flour

½ cup old-fashioned
rolled oats

¼ teaspoon
ground cinnamon

Pinch of kosher salt

⅓ cup pine nuts,
toasted (page 246)

4 tablespoons cold
unsalted butter,
cut into small pieces,
plus more for pan

FOR THE FILLING

4 apricots, pitted and cut
into sixths (about 2 cups)

12 ounces strawberries
(about 15), hulled and
halved, or quartered if
large (about 2½ cups)

½ cup granulated sugar

2 teaspoons
fresh lemon juice

1 teaspoon cornstarch

Pinch of kosher salt

1. Make the topping: In a medium bowl, mix brown sugar, flour, oats, cinnamon, salt, and toasted pine nuts until combined. With your fingertips, work in butter until small clumps form. Refrigerate mixture until cold, at least 30 minutes or up to overnight.

2. Make the filling: Preheat oven to 350°F. Butter a 9½-inch shallow round baking dish. In a medium bowl, combine apricots, strawberries, granulated sugar, lemon juice, cornstarch, and salt.

3. Transfer filling to prepared baking dish and top evenly with crumble. Bake until bubbling in center and crumble is browned, about 40 minutes. Transfer to a wire rack to cool at least 20 minutes before serving.

TIP:
The pine-nut topping
freezes well, so you
can double it and
freeze half, to have
on hand when
friends (or cravings)
come calling.

STRAWBERRY TARTLETS WITH YOGURT CREAM

For a French pastry cream with a little extra brightness, we substituted yogurt for the usual milk. The result is as silky as ever, but with an addicting tanginess that enhances this dessert's flaky, buttery shell and sweet berries. **MAKES 9**

FOR THE YOGURT CREAM

⅓ cup sugar

2 tablespoons cornstarch

¼ tablespoon kosher salt

1⅓ cups plain
whole-milk yogurt

2 large egg yolks

2 tablespoons
unsalted butter

FOR THE TARTLETS

Unbleached all-purpose
flour, for dusting

1 package (14 ounces)
all-butter puff pastry,
such as Dufour, thawed

¼ cup sugar

2 cups sliced strawberries

1 teaspoon
fresh lemon juice

Pinch of kosher salt

¼ cup cold heavy cream

1. Make the yogurt cream: In a medium saucepan, off heat, whisk together sugar, cornstarch, and salt. Whisk in yogurt and egg yolks. Add butter and cook over medium, stirring with a rubber spatula, until mixture comes to a boil, about 7 minutes. Let boil, stirring constantly, 1 minute. Transfer to a medium bowl. Cover with plastic wrap, pressing it directly onto surface to prevent skin from forming. Refrigerate at least 2 hours or up to 1 day. Just before using, whisk until smooth.

2. Make the tartlets: Preheat oven to 400°F with racks in upper and lower thirds. Lightly dust work surface and puff pastry sheet with flour; roll out puff pastry to slightly less than ¼ inch thick. Sprinkle with 2 tablespoons sugar, pressing and rolling sugar so as much sticks as possible. Trim pastry sheet to a 9-by-12-inch rectangle, then cut nine 3-by-4-inch rectangles. Score a ½-inch border around each rectangle, being careful not to cut all the way through. Score center pieces diagonally at ½-inch intervals for a decorative top, if desired.

3. Transfer rectangles to a parchment-lined baking sheet; freeze 15 minutes. Bake on top rack 15 minutes, then transfer to bottom rack; bake until caramelized, about 10 minutes more. Transfer to a wire rack to cool 10 minutes. Using scissors, cut center of tops away and reserve; let cool.

4. In a small bowl, combine strawberries, remaining 2 tablespoons sugar, the lemon juice, and salt; let stand 10 minutes. In a medium bowl, whisk heavy cream to soft peaks. Fold whipped cream into yogurt cream. Divide among tartlets and top with berries. Serve with reserved tops.

STRAWBERRY-PISTACHIO SEMIFREDDO

Next time you're looking for a refreshing dessert to serve at a dinner party, consider a semifreddo. It combines the richness of ice cream and the lush, airy texture of frozen mousse. Maybe the best part? Your mixer and freezer do all the work—no ice-cream maker required. **SERVES 12**

½ cup unsalted roasted shelled pistachios

8 ounces strawberries, hulled (about 2 cups), plus more, hulled and sliced, for serving (optional)

½ cup plus 3 tablespoons sugar

3 large egg yolks, room temperature

1½ cups cold heavy cream

½ teaspoon vanilla extract

1. Line a standard 5-by-9-inch loaf pan with plastic wrap, leaving a 2-inch overhang on all sides. Pulse pistachios in a food processor until coarsely chopped (some will break down to a coarse grind). Transfer to a small bowl (do not wipe processor clean). Place strawberries and 3 tablespoons sugar in processor and purée until smooth. Transfer to a fine-mesh sieve set over a medium bowl. Strain purée, pressing on solids to extract as much liquid as possible; discard solids.

2. Prepare an ice-water bath. Combine egg yolks and remaining ½ cup sugar in a bowl set over (not in) a pot of simmering water. Using an electric mixer on high speed, beat until pale yellow and tripled in volume, about 3 minutes. Transfer to ice bath and stir until mixture is very thick and cool, about 3 minutes.

3. In a large bowl, beat together cream and vanilla until soft peaks form. Whisk one-third of whipped cream into egg mixture, whisking until smooth. Fold into remaining cream with a rubber spatula just until thoroughly incorporated.

4. Pour half the cream mixture into strawberry purée. Gently fold together until thoroughly incorporated, then pour into loaf pan and smooth top. Fold pistachios into remaining cream mixture and pour evenly over strawberry cream; smooth top. Fold plastic wrap over surface and freeze at least 12 hours and up to 3 days.

5. To serve, peel plastic from surface. Invert pan onto a cutting board. Unmold semifreddo, remove plastic, and cut crosswise into ¾-inch-thick slices. Serve with sliced strawberries, if desired.

SUMMER

You almost can't pick fast enough. Stone fruits, cherries, and berries appear, ripen, and are gathered at their delicious peak. Bake with whatever you can resist eating out of hand, letting them dazzle in pavlovas, pies, cakes, and galettes.

TIP:
Bake until the
filling is bubbling.
This is how you
know the starch has
been activated,
so the juices will
be pleasingly
thick, not watery.

PLUM-BLACKBERRY COBBLER

This delectable fruit combo of ripe, sweet plums and blackberries gets enhanced by black pepper and Chinese five-spice powder—a warm mix of cloves, star anise, fennel, Szechuan pepper, and cinnamon. Wait for the last ten minutes to top with the prebaked puff pastry, so it absorbs some juice but stays crisp. **SERVES 8**

FOR THE CRUST

1 package (14 ounces) all-butter puff pastry, such as Dufour, thawed if frozen

Unbleached all-purpose flour, for dusting

1 large egg white, lightly beaten, for egg wash

Coarse sanding sugar, for sprinkling

FOR THE FILLING

1¼ pounds black plums (8 to 9 medium), pitted and cut into ¾-inch-thick wedges (about 4 cups)

6 ounces blackberries (about 1¼ cups)

½ cup granulated sugar

3 tablespoons cornstarch

¼ teaspoon Chinese five-spice powder

¼ teaspoon kosher salt

Pinch of freshly ground pepper

1. Make the crust: Preheat oven to 375°F with racks in upper and bottom thirds. Unfold pastry on lightly floured parchment and roll out to ⅛-inch thickness. Gently set a 9-inch ovenproof pie dish, upside down (do not press down), on 1 side of pastry and cut around dish using a sharp paring knife. Remove dish. Cut five ¾-inch-wide strips from scraps to lay across crust.

2. Brush pastry round with beaten egg white (do not let drip down sides). Adhere strips to surface, starting in center and working out toward the edge, spacing them evenly; brush again with egg wash. Cut out a 2½-inch hole in center of pastry round using a biscuit cutter (sprinkle cutout with sugar and bake for a snack). Sprinkle pastry round with sanding sugar. Transfer pastry on parchment to a baking sheet and freeze for 15 minutes.

3. Make the filling: In a large bowl, mix together plums, blackberries, granulated sugar, cornstarch, five-spice powder, salt, and pepper. Pour filling into pie dish and cover with parchment-lined foil. Transfer to a foil-lined rimmed baking sheet.

4. Bake pastry crust on top rack and filling in bottom third of oven for 30 minutes. Transfer crust on baking sheet to a wire rack (it should be golden and cooked through) to cool slightly. Continue to bake filling until starting to bubble in center, about 30 minutes more. Remove from oven, uncover, and top with pastry crust.

5. Return cobbler to oven and bake until bubbling vigorously in center, about 10 minutes more. Transfer cobbler to a wire rack to cool for at least 1 hour before serving.

PEACH PAVLOVA

Peaches and cream, meet pavlova. This cloudlike dessert of toasty meringue—crisp on the outside, light and tender inside—is typically filled with whipped cream and berries. Here, sunny peach halves, poached in vanilla-scented liquid, make a sensational stand-in. **SERVES 6**

FOR THE PAVLOVA

4 large egg whites, room temperature

¾ cup packed light-brown sugar

Pinch of kosher salt

¼ cup granulated sugar

1 teaspoon distilled white vinegar

1 teaspoon vanilla paste or extract

FOR THE POACHED PEACHES

1 cup granulated sugar

¼ cup fresh lemon juice (from 2 lemons)

1 teaspoon vanilla paste or extract

3 peaches (1 pound), halved and pitted

FOR THE TOPPING

1 cup cold heavy cream

1 tablespoon granulated sugar

Mint leaves, for garnish

1. Make the pavlova: Preheat oven to 300°F with a rack in center. Line a baking sheet with parchment. Using an overturned bowl as a guide, trace an 8-inch circle on parchment; turn parchment marked-side down. Place egg whites, brown sugar, and salt in the bowl of a mixer fitted with the whisk attachment. Beat on low until combined. Increase speed to medium; beat until soft peaks form, about 9 minutes. With mixer running, add granulated sugar. Continue beating until peaks are stiff and glossy, about 2 minutes. Beat in vinegar and vanilla.

2. Adhere corners of marked parchment to baking sheet with dollops of meringue. Using a rubber spatula, spread remaining meringue within marked 8-inch circle; form peaks around edge and a well in center. Bake until meringue is crisp around edges and just set in center, about 1 hour 15 minutes. Turn off heat and let cool in oven about 2 hours. Transfer baking sheet to wire rack until meringue is cool enough to handle. Peel meringue off parchment; let cool completely on rack.

3. Make the poached peaches: Prepare an ice-water bath. In a large saucepan, combine granulated sugar, lemon juice, vanilla, and 2¼ cups water. Bring to a simmer over medium-high heat and cook, stirring, until sugar dissolves. Add peaches, cut-side up, and cover with a parchment round to keep submerged. Reduce heat to low and simmer until peaches are tender when pierced with the tip of a knife, 8 to 10 minutes. Using a slotted spoon, transfer peaches to a plate. When cool enough to handle, peel and discard skins. Bring poaching liquid to a boil; cook until thickened and reduced by half (you should have 1 cup), about 10 minutes. Transfer to a bowl and chill in ice bath until cold.

4. Make the topping: Beat heavy cream with granulated sugar until stiff peaks form. Place meringue on a serving platter. Spoon whipped cream on top, spreading to edges. Add peaches, cut-side down. Drizzle with syrup, sprinkle with mint, and serve.

TIP:

After poaching the fruit, don't discard the extra syrupy liquid. Decant it into a bottle and keep in the fridge, up to a month, to add a quick hit of peachy nectar to cocktails, iced tea, or seltzer.

LEMON CAKE WITH RASPBERRY–CREAM CHEESE FROSTING

A pink-tinted cream cheese frosting blankets this citrusy single-layer treat; it gets its flavor and that pretty hue from freeze-dried berries. Fresh berries get scattered on top. We won't blame you if you can't wait for dessert with this one—a slice is just right with afternoon tea. **SERVES 10 TO 12**

FOR THE CAKE

1½ sticks unsalted butter, room temperature, plus more for pan

2 cups unbleached all-purpose flour, plus more for pan

1 teaspoon baking powder

½ teaspoon baking soda

1 teaspoon kosher salt

⅔ cup whole milk

1 tablespoon finely grated lemon zest plus ⅓ cup fresh juice (2 lemons)

1 cup granulated sugar

2 teaspoons vanilla extract or paste

2 large eggs, room temperature

FOR THE FROSTING

6 ounces cream cheese, room temperature

6 tablespoons unsalted butter, room temperature

1 cup plus 2 tablespoons confectioners' sugar, sifted

¼ ounce freeze-dried raspberries (⅓ cup), finely ground

2 cups fresh raspberries

1. Make the cake: Preheat oven to 350°F. Brush a 9-inch round cake pan with butter. Line bottom with parchment; brush with butter. Dust with flour, tapping out any excess.

2. In a medium bowl, whisk together flour, baking powder, baking soda, and salt. In a small bowl, stir together milk and lemon juice. With an electric mixer on medium speed, beat butter with lemon zest, granulated sugar, and vanilla in a large bowl until light and fluffy, 3 to 4 minutes. Beat in eggs, one at a time.

3. Reduce speed to low and beat in flour mixture in three batches, alternating with milk mixture and beginning and ending with flour mixture, just until no dry flour remains (do not overmix). Transfer batter to prepared pan, smoothing top with a small offset spatula. Bake until cake is golden and springs back when gently pressed, about 40 minutes. Transfer pan to a wire rack to cool 20 minutes. Turn out cake onto rack, remove parchment, and let cool completely.

4. Make the frosting: With a mixer on medium speed, beat cream cheese and butter in a medium bowl until light and fluffy, 2 to 3 minutes. Beat in confectioners' sugar and freeze-dried berries until smooth. Spread frosting over top of cake. Decorate with fresh berries. (Cake is best served on the day it's made but can be refrigerated in an airtight container up to 2 days.)

BLUEBERRY PIE WITH LATTICE-WEAVE CRUST

The deep purple-blue filling of this blueberry pie bubbles through the woven crust like a delicious little wink. It's an impressive presentation, but once you know the technique (hint: create the lattice on parchment, then chill before topping the pie), it's surprisingly easy. **SERVES 8**

Unbleached all-purpose flour, for dusting

2 disks Pâte Brisée (page 236)

FOR THE FILLING

3 pints fresh blueberries (6 cups)

Finely grated zest of 1 lemon plus 1 tablespoon fresh juice

½ cup granulated sugar

3 tablespoons cornstarch

¼ teaspoon kosher salt

¼ teaspoon ground cinnamon

2 tablespoons unsalted butter, cut into pieces

1 egg, lightly beaten, for egg wash

Coarse sanding sugar, for decorating

1. On a lightly floured surface, roll out 1 disk of dough to a 13-inch round; fit into a 9-inch pie dish. Refrigerate while making lattice. Roll out a second disk of dough to an 11-inch square. Trim edges, then cut square into eleven ½- to 1-inch-wide strips.

2. Assemble lattice on a parchment-lined unrimmed baking sheet. You will be alternating between double strips of dough and a single strip to create this pattern. Lay 2 strips, touching one another, diagonally across the center of the parchment. Lay another strip on top of the 2 strips, going diagonally in the opposite direction. Continue weaving, following the pattern of double and single strips in opposite diagonal directions. You will need to fold back double strips as you work to lay the single strips, then unfold them to weave a lattice pattern. Transfer sheet to freezer until lattice is well chilled, about 30 minutes.

3. Preheat oven to 425°F with a rack in center. Line a rimmed baking sheet with foil and place on rack to preheat.

4. Make the filling: In a medium bowl, gently toss together blueberries, lemon zest and juice, granulated sugar, cornstarch, salt, cinnamon, and butter. Transfer blueberry mixture to prepared pie dish. Brush edges of crust with egg wash. Place chilled lattice over filling; press edges to seal with bottom crust. Using kitchen shears, trim dough to a 1-inch overhang. Tuck overhang under so edges are flush with rim. Brush lattice with egg wash and sprinkle with sanding sugar.

5. Bake on preheated baking sheet 20 minutes, then reduce oven temperature to 375°F and continue baking until filling is bubbling and crust is evenly browned (if browning too quickly, tent edges with foil), 1 hour to 1 hour 15 minutes. Transfer to a wire rack and let cool completely before serving.

PEACH-CARDAMOM UPSIDE-DOWN CAKE

*Summer peaches—highlighted here in an upside-down sheet cake—
reveal a whole new side of themselves when you add just a hint of unexpected
seasoning. A quarter teaspoon of cardamom will do the job, plus a pinch
of saffron if you have it. Alternatively, cinnamon always works,
or even black pepper.* **SERVES 12 TO 16**

1 stick (½ cup)
unsalted butter, room
temperature, plus
3 tablespoons cut into
pieces, plus more for pan

1¼ pounds firm but
ripe peaches (5 to 6
medium), pitted and
cut into ¼-inch-thick
wedges (4 cups)

1⅔ cups sugar

2 teaspoons
fresh lemon juice

1½ teaspoons kosher salt

1½ cups unbleached
all-purpose flour

⅓ cup finely
ground cornmeal

2 teaspoons
baking powder

¼ teaspoon
ground cardamom

Pinch of saffron (optional)

¾ cup whole milk

2 large eggs

1. Preheat oven to 350°F. Butter a 9-by-13-inch baking pan or
rimmed baking sheet. Dot with the cut-up 3 tablespoons butter.
In a large bowl, toss peaches with ⅓ cup sugar, the lemon juice,
and ¼ teaspoon salt. Spread evenly into pan.

2. In a large bowl, whisk together flour, cornmeal, baking powder, remaining 1¼ teaspoons salt, and the cardamom. In a small
bowl, sprinkle saffron, if desired, over milk. With an electric
mixer on medium speed, beat remaining 1 stick (½ cup) butter
and 1⅓ cups sugar in a large bowl until pale and fluffy, about
3 minutes. Beat in eggs, one at a time, beating well after each
addition. Beat in flour mixture in two batches, alternating with
milk, until smooth. Spread evenly over peaches.

3. Bake until golden and a cake tester comes out clean, 45 to
50 minutes. Let cool 45 minutes. Run a knife around edge of cake
and invert onto a platter to serve. Let cool to room temperature,
about 1 hour. (Cake is best eaten the day it's made but can be
wrapped well and refrigerated for up to 1 day; return to room
temperature before serving.)

SOUR CHERRY CRUMBLE BARS

Tucked into a lunchbox or nibbled on while standing at the kitchen counter, these buttery, fruity bars are the perfect out-of-hand snack. Sour cherries make the flavor here, pleasantly balancing the sweetness of the crust, so seek them out. **SERVES 9**

FOR THE CRUST

1 stick (½ cup) plus
5 tablespoons unsalted
butter, room temperature,
plus more for pan

1 cup sugar

2 cups unbleached
all-purpose flour

1 teaspoon kosher salt

FOR THE FILLING

1 pound sour cherries
(3 cups), pitted

¾ cup sugar

2 tablespoons unbleached
all-purpose flour

1 tablespoon
fresh lemon juice

½ teaspoon kosher salt

1. Preheat oven to 375°F. Butter an 8-inch square cake pan. Line with parchment, leaving a 2-inch overhang on two sides; butter parchment.

2. Make the crust: With an electric mixer on medium-high, beat butter with sugar in a medium bowl until pale and fluffy, about 3 minutes, scraping down bowl as needed. Reduce speed to medium-low, add flour and salt, and beat until dough forms clumps but does not completely hold together. Press 2½ cups flour mixture into bottom and 1 inch up sides of prepared pan.

3. Make the filling: In a medium bowl, stir together cherries, sugar, flour, lemon juice, and salt. Pour into crust. Crumble remaining flour mixture (about ½ cup) evenly over top, squeezing to create clumps.

4. Bake until bubbling in center and crust is golden, about 1 hour 10 minutes (if browning too quickly, tent top with foil). Transfer to a wire rack to cool at least 20 minutes before slicing into 9 squares.

STONE FRUIT GALETTE WITH CORNMEAL CRUST

A bit of cornmeal gives the crust of this free-form tart a textured edge that nicely complements the sweet filling. Peaches, apricots, or any ripe stone fruit work well here; just adjust the sugar to suit the tartness of the fruit (up to a half cup for tart apricots). **SERVES 8**

FOR THE CRUST

1¼ cups unbleached all-purpose flour

¼ cup finely ground yellow cornmeal

1 teaspoon granulated sugar

½ teaspoon kosher salt

1 stick (½ cup) cold unsalted butter, cut into pieces

3 to 5 tablespoons ice-cold water

FOR THE FILLING

1½ pounds peaches or apricots, pitted and sliced into ½-inch-thick wedges (4¾ cups)

⅓ to ½ cup granulated sugar

1 teaspoon fresh lemon juice

¼ teaspoon kosher salt

1 tablespoon cornstarch

Unbleached all-purpose flour, for dusting

1 large egg, lightly beaten, for egg wash

Fine sanding sugar, for sprinkling

Whipped Cream (page 246), for serving

1. Make the crust: Pulse flour, cornmeal, granulated sugar, and salt in a food processor. Add butter and pulse until mixture resembles coarse meal, with a few pea-size pieces of butter remaining. Drizzle with 3 tablespoons ice water. Pulse until dough just begins to hold together. If dough is too dry, add up to 2 tablespoons more water, 1 to 2 teaspoons at a time. Don't overmix. Shape dough into a disk and wrap in plastic. Refrigerate until well chilled, at least 1 hour and up to 2 days.

2. Make the filling: Preheat oven to 375°F. In a large bowl, stir together fruit, granulated sugar to taste, lemon juice, salt, and cornstarch.

3. On a lightly floured piece of parchment, roll out crust to a 13-inch round, about ⅛ inch thick. Transfer on parchment to a baking sheet. Arrange fruit in center, leaving a 2-inch border. Fold border over to enclose fruit, leaving center open. Brush crust with egg wash, brushing under folds to help seal, and sprinkle with sanding sugar.

4. Bake until golden brown and bubbling in center, about 1 hour 10 minutes. Let cool on baking sheet 10 minutes. Transfer galette on parchment to a wire rack to cool completely. Serve with whipped cream.

RASPBERRY–CHOCOLATE MOUSSE PIE

Raspberries and dark chocolate are a true love match. Here, one pound of the sweet, deep-pink berries are showcased against a rich chocolate mousse. Buy the best-quality chocolate you can for this filling–the berries (and you) deserve it. **SERVES 8 TO 10**

FOR THE CRUST

1¼ cups unbleached all-purpose flour, plus more for dusting

⅓ cup sugar

2 tablespoons unsweetened Dutch-process cocoa powder

½ teaspoon kosher salt

6 tablespoons cold unsalted butter, cut into small pieces

3 large egg yolks

1 teaspoon vanilla extract

FOR THE FILLING

6 large egg yolks

⅓ cup sugar

¼ teaspoon kosher salt

6 ounces bittersweet chocolate, coarsely chopped (about 1 cup)

1¼ cups cold heavy cream

FOR THE TOPPING

1 pound raspberries (4 cups)

½ cup sugar

2 tablespoons cornstarch

Pinch of kosher salt

1. Make the crust: Pulse flour, sugar, cocoa, and salt in a food processor until combined. Add butter and pulse until mixture resembles coarse meal, with a few pea-size pieces of butter remaining, about 10 seconds. Add egg yolks and vanilla, and process until mixture just begins to hold together (no longer than 30 seconds). Shape dough into a disk. Wrap in plastic and refrigerate until firm, at least 1 hour or up to 2 days.

2. Preheat oven to 375°F. On a lightly floured surface, roll out dough to ⅛-inch thickness. Fit dough into a 9-inch pie dish and, using kitchen shears, trim excess dough flush with rim. Cut edge of dough ½ inch deep at ¾-inch intervals; bend every other section back toward the center. Pierce bottom of dough all over with a fork. Freeze 15 minutes. Line crust with parchment and fill with dried beans or pie weights. Bake until edges are set, about 20 minutes. Carefully remove parchment and beans. Bake crust until bottom is dry, about 10 minutes more. Transfer to a wire rack to cool completely.

3. Make the filling: In a heatproof bowl set over (not in) a pot of simmering water, whisk together egg yolks, sugar, and salt until sugar dissolves. Stir in bittersweet chocolate until just melted. Let cool 10 minutes. In a medium bowl, beat cream with an electric mixer on medium-high speed until medium-stiff peaks form. Whisk one-third of whipped cream into chocolate mixture. Fold in remaining whipped cream. Pour mixture into crust. Refrigerate at least 3 hours.

4. Make the topping: In a medium saucepan, combine 1 cup raspberries, the sugar, cornstarch, and salt, crushing berries to release some juice. Stir in ⅓ cup water and bring to a boil. Continue to boil, stirring, until mixture is thick, 2 to 3 minutes. Strain through a fine-mesh sieve into a large bowl; discard seeds. Let cool 5 minutes. Add remaining 3 cups raspberries and gently stir to coat. Let stand 15 minutes to cool slightly, then spoon over pie. Refrigerate 15 to 30 minutes before serving.

TIP:
Leftovers needn't go to waste. Make smaller tarts with extra puff pastry dough after cutting: Use two or three pieces of stone fruit and bake about 20 minutes. The leftover frangipane is a great addition to French toast batter.

TARTS WITH STONE FRUITS AND FRANGIPANE

Reach for peaches, plums, apricots—or really any stone fruit that looks best this week. Layer slices over creamy frangipane, an uncomplicated almond filling that partners flawlessly with buttery, flaky pastry. **SERVES 6**

½ cup blanched whole almonds

¼ cup granulated sugar

4 tablespoons unsalted butter, room temperature

2 large eggs, room temperature

Pinch of kosher salt

Pinch of ground cinnamon

Unbleached all-purpose flour, for dusting

1 package (14 ounces) all-butter puff pastry, preferably Dufour, thawed

1 pound assorted stone fruits, such as apricots, peaches, nectarines, and plums, pitted and cut into ½-inch slices

2 tablespoons turbinado sugar

Unsprayed fresh edible flowers, such as micro marigolds, for serving (optional)

1. Pulse almonds in a food processor until finely ground. Add granulated sugar, butter, 1 egg, salt, and cinnamon; process until smooth.

2. Preheat oven to 400°F. Whisk remaining egg with 1 tablespoon water. On a lightly floured surface, roll out puff pastry to an 8-by-12-inch rectangle, about ⅛ inch thick. Cut pastry into six 4-inch squares and transfer to a parchment-lined baking sheet. Brush edges of pastry squares with egg wash. Spread 2 teaspoons almond mixture in center of each square; top with 4 pieces fruit. Sprinkle each tart with some turbinado sugar.

3. Bake until tarts are golden brown and fruit is soft, 22 to 25 minutes. Let cool on a wire rack, 20 minutes. Sprinkle with flowers, if desired, and serve.

BERRIES AND CHERRIES ICE-CREAM CAKE

Mixed berries, with a chocolate-wafer crust and a sensational dark-chocolate shell, make for a memorable ice-cream cake. Use any berries you like; macerating in vodka and sugar prevents them from becoming hard once frozen and gives them polished appeal. **SERVES 12**

6 ounces vodka

⅔ cup sugar

5 ounces fresh sweet cherries (1 cup), pitted and halved, plus more for serving

9 ounces fresh berries (1½ cups), such as raspberries and blackberries, plus more for serving

9 ounces chocolate wafers (about 42), such as Nabisco Famous

4 tablespoons unsalted butter, melted

½ teaspoon kosher salt

1 pint cherry ice cream

1½ cups cold heavy cream

1 pint vanilla ice cream

5 ounces semisweet chocolate, chopped

1. In a pitcher or bowl, combine vodka and ⅓ cup sugar; gently stir in cherries and berries. Let stand 2 hours, stirring occasionally, or refrigerate, covered, up to 12 hours. Strain (reserve syrup for another use; see Tip).

2. Pulse wafers in a food processor until finely ground. Add butter and salt; pulse until mixture has the texture of wet sand. Press half of mixture into the bottom of a 9-inch springform pan and freeze until firm, about 30 minutes.

3. Temper cherry ice cream in refrigerator until it has texture of soft-serve, about 20 minutes. Meanwhile, with an electric mixer on high speed, beat cream with remaining ⅓ cup sugar in a medium bowl to soft peaks. Stir two-thirds of whipped cream (refrigerate remainder) into cherry ice cream to combine. Pour ice-cream mixture over crust; smooth top and freeze until firm, about 1 hour.

4. Top with remaining crumb mixture; press to lightly pack. Freeze 20 minutes. Meanwhile, temper vanilla ice cream in the refrigerator about 20 minutes, then stir into remaining whipped cream just to combine. Fold in half of cherry-berry mixture. Spread over crumb mixture, smooth top, and sprinkle with remaining cherry-berry mixture. Cover and freeze at least 4 hours or up to 2 days.

5. In a heatproof bowl set over (not in) a pot of boiling water, melt chocolate. Let cool until no longer hot but still pourable, about 10 minutes. Run a thin-bladed knife between cake and sides of pan to loosen; remove sides. Run knife between bottom of cake and pan; transfer to a cake plate. Drizzle chocolate evenly over cake; top with whole cherries and berries, if desired.

6. Return to freezer until chocolate hardens, 2 to 3 minutes (or freeze, loosely covered, up to 8 hours). Slice into wedges using a sharp knife dipped in hot water (if cake is too firm to slice, let temper in the refrigerator 10 to 15 minutes first).

TIP:
After straining
the macerated berries,
save the vodka to
liven up a summery
cocktail.

HAND PIES, TWO WAYS

Individual, portable portions of buttery crust and tasty fruit filling, hand pies are a quintessential picnic dessert. Use peak-season fruit and fry them for a shatteringly crisp finish (like the peach pies here) or bake them for a slightly more virtuous but every bit as irresistible option (page 186). **SERVES 8**

FRIED PEACH HAND PIES

FOR THE CRUST

3 cups unbleached all-purpose flour, plus more for dusting

1 tablespoon sugar

2 teaspoons kosher salt

1 teaspoon baking powder

1 stick (½ cup) cold unsalted butter, cut into pieces

⅓ cup chilled vegetable shortening

½ cup ice water, plus more if needed

FOR THE FILLING

1½ pounds ripe peaches (4 to 6 medium)

¾ cup plus 2 tablespoons sugar

1 tablespoon plus 2 teaspoons cornstarch

1 tablespoon plus 1 teaspoon fresh lemon juice

½ teaspoon kosher salt

½ teaspoon ground allspice

½ teaspoon ground cinnamon

Vegetable oil, for frying

1. Make the crust: Pulse flour, sugar, salt, and baking powder in a food processor. Add butter and shortening and pulse until mixture resembles coarse crumbs, with a few pea-size pieces of butter remaining. Drizzle with ½ cup water and pulse until dough is crumbly but holds together when squeezed (if necessary, add up to 1 tablespoon more water, 1 teaspoon at a time). Don't overmix. Divide dough and shape into 2 rectangles. Wrap each in plastic and refrigerate until firm, 1 hour.

2. Make the filling: Bring a large pot of water to a boil. Prepare an ice-water bath. Cut an X in the bottom of each peach. Drop in boiling water and cook just until skin begins to peel back, about 30 seconds. Transfer to ice bath to stop cooking. Peel peaches, pit, and cut into ½-inch pieces (you should have 3 cups). In a medium saucepan, combine peaches, 6 tablespoons sugar, the cornstarch, lemon juice, salt, and allspice. Let stand 30 minutes.

3. Bring peach mixture to a simmer over medium-high. Cook, stirring until juices are thickened, about 1 minute. Transfer peach mixture to a baking sheet. Let cool to room temperature. In a shallow bowl or large plate, combine remaining ½ cup sugar and the cinnamon.

4. On a lightly floured surface, roll out one piece of dough to a 9½-by-11-inch rectangle. Trim edges and cut into four 4¾-by-5½-inch rectangles. Place 2 heaping tablespoons filling on one side of each rectangle. Fold dough over to enclose filling. Press edges to seal. Refrigerate until chilled, about 15 minutes. Repeat with remaining dough and filling.

5. Set a wire rack in a rimmed baking sheet. Heat 1½ to 1¾ inches oil in a deep heavy pot over medium heat until an instant-read thermometer registers 350°F. Add 2 hand pies to oil and fry, maintaining a temperature between 350°F and 360°F, turning occasionally, until deep golden brown, 5 to 6 minutes total. Transfer to wire rack with a slotted spoon and let cool for 5 minutes. Toss in bowl of cinnamon sugar to coat. Repeat with remaining hand pies.

BAKED BLACKBERRY HAND PIES

FOR THE CRUST

1 tablespoon sour cream

1 tablespoon
fresh lemon juice

2 to 3 tablespoons
ice-cold water

1¼ cups unbleached
all-purpose flour,
plus more for dusting

¾ teaspoon kosher salt

⅓ cup plus 1 teaspoon
granulated sugar

1 stick (½ cup)
cold unsalted butter,
cut into pieces

FOR THE FILLING

¾ cup fresh blackberries
(about 3 ounces)

¾ cup fresh raspberries
(about 3 ounces)

1 tablespoon plus
1½ teaspoons cornstarch

1 large egg, lightly beaten,
for egg wash

Fine sanding sugar,
for sprinkling

1. Make the crust: In a small bowl, whisk together sour cream, lemon juice, and 2 tablespoons ice water. In a large bowl, mix together flour, ½ teaspoon salt, and 1 teaspoon granulated sugar. Add cold butter and, with an electric mixer on medium-low speed, beat until mixture resembles coarse meal with some pea-size pieces of butter remaining. Gradually beat in sour-cream mixture until just combined but still crumbly. (Squeeze a small amount of dough to make sure it holds together. If dough is too dry, add up to 1 tablespoon more ice water, 1 teaspoon at a time.) Divide dough in half, shape into 2 flat rectangles, and wrap each in plastic. Refrigerate just until firm, about 45 minutes.

2. With a floured rolling pin, roll out each piece of dough into a 7-by-14-inch rectangle on floured parchment. (Dough will be very thin.) Transfer dough on parchment to 2 baking sheets and refrigerate until firm, about 15 minutes.

3. Make the filling: In a medium bowl, stir together berries, remaining ⅓ cup granulated sugar and ¼ teaspoon salt, and the cornstarch. Slide 1 chilled piece of dough, still on parchment, onto a work surface. With a long side facing you, cut dough crosswise into four 3½-by-7-inch strips.

4. Mound 2 tablespoons berry mixture in center of bottom half of each strip. Brush edges with egg wash and fold top half over fruit to enclose. Press firmly to seal and trim bottom edge, leaving folded top edge uncut. Cut two vents in the center of each hand pie. Transfer to a baking sheet lined with parchment, spacing each about 2 inches apart. Freeze until firm, at least 45 minutes. Repeat with remaining dough and berry mixture.

5. Preheat oven to 375°F with racks in upper and lower thirds. Lightly brush hand pies with egg wash and sprinkle with sanding sugar. Bake, rotating sheets and switching racks halfway through, until pies are golden brown, 35 to 40 minutes. Transfer to a wire rack to cool. Serve warm or at room temperature.

RED-FRUIT PAVLOVA

A crisp and marshmallowy meringue is the ideal vessel for any number of gorgeous fruits. Here, the theme is red and more red: Sour cherry jam, strawberries, and whipped cream fill the shell, then more fruits are piled on top. **SERVES 8**

4 large egg whites, room temperature

Kosher salt

1⅓ cups superfine sugar

3 teaspoons distilled white vinegar

1 teaspoon cornstarch

8 ounces sour cherries (1 cup), pitted and chopped

3 ounces strawberries, hulled and coarsely chopped (½ cup)

1¼ cups cold heavy cream

2 tablespoons confectioners' sugar

1 pound mixed red fruits, such as whole or quartered strawberries, whole raspberries, and pitted sweet cherries, for serving (2½ cups)

1. Preheat oven to 300°F with a rack in center. Line a rimmed baking sheet with parchment. With an electric mixer on medium-high speed, whisk egg whites and a pinch of salt until soft peaks form, 1 to 2 minutes. With mixer running, gradually add 1 cup superfine sugar. Continue beating until stiff, glossy peaks form, 6 to 8 minutes more. Fold in 2 teaspoons vinegar and the cornstarch.

2. Adhere corners of parchment to prepared pan with dollops of meringue. Dollop meringue in center of pan. With a small offset spatula, form a 6½-by-9½-inch rectangle, with a 1½-inch-tall border around edges and a well in center. Bake until meringue starts to feel crisp and take on color, 45 minutes. Reduce temperature to 250°F and bake until it lifts off parchment easily, about 30 minutes more. Transfer on parchment to a wire rack until meringue is cool enough to handle, about 15 minutes. Separate from parchment, but leave on rack to cool completely, about 1 hour. (Note: It may crack a bit as it settles.)

3. In a small saucepan, combine sour cherries, strawberries, remaining ⅓ cup superfine sugar and 1 teaspoon vinegar, and a pinch of salt. Bring to a boil and cook until fruit breaks down and mixture thickens to a jam, 10 to 15 minutes. (You should have ½ cup jam.) Let cool.

4. In a medium bowl, whip cream and 2 tablespoons confectioners' sugar with a mixer on medium-high speed to soft peaks. Swirl ¼ cup jam into cream. Dollop cream into well of pavlova. Garnish with fresh fruit. Serve with additional jam served on the side, if desired.

NECTARINE CLAFOUTI

Reminiscent of a Dutch baby pancake, this is one of Martha's favorite ways to showcase in-season fruit. The clafouti's eggy, vanilla-scented batter puffs up gorgeously as it bakes around fruit (cherries are classic, but nectarines are delightful here). Timing is everything with this light dessert, since it's best served warm from the oven. **SERVES 8**

3 to 4 ripe nectarines
(about 1 pound)

1 cup whole milk

1 cup heavy cream

4 large whole eggs
plus 2 large egg yolks

1 vanilla bean, split
and seeds scraped

¼ cup granulated sugar

2 tablespoons unbleached
all-purpose flour

¼ teaspoon kosher salt

1 tablespoon unsalted
butter, room temperature

Confectioners' sugar,
for sprinkling

1. Preheat oven to 375°F with a 10-inch round baking dish (1½ to 2 inches deep) on center rack.

2. Bring a small pot of water to a boil. With a sharp knife, cut a shallow X into bottom of each nectarine. Add to pot and blanch 30 to 40 seconds. When cool enough to handle, use a paring knife to remove and discard skin and pit and cut each nectarine into ¼-inch slices.

3. Purée milk, cream, eggs, yolks, vanilla seeds, granulated sugar, flour, and salt in a blender until smooth, about 2 minutes. Strain through a fine-mesh sieve into a liquid-measuring cup.

4. Carefully remove preheated baking dish from oven and brush with butter (caution: it will sizzle). Immediately pour in just enough batter to coat bottom of dish. Return to oven and bake until golden brown, about 5 minutes.

5. Pour in remaining batter and arrange nectarines in a single layer, covering as much surface area as possible. Return to oven and bake until puffed and browned, 35 to 40 minutes more. Let cool slightly. Dust with confectioners' sugar and serve.

SOUR CHERRY PIE

The season for sour cherries goes by in a blink; don't miss your chance to grab it. (Although, if you do, frozen ones, well thawed and drained before weighing, can make a fine substitute.) Embellish this simple pie with twisted strips of pâte brisée, in different widths, for an eye-catching top crust. **SERVES 8**

2 pounds fresh
sour cherries,
pitted (6 cups)

1 cup granulated sugar

¼ cup cornstarch

½ teaspoon
vanilla extract

2 disks Pâte Brisée
(page 236)

Unbleached all-purpose
flour, for dusting

2 tablespoons
unsalted butter,
cut into small pieces

1 large egg

2 tablespoons
heavy cream

Coarse sanding sugar,
for sprinkling

Whipped Cream
(page 246), for serving

1. Preheat oven to 375°F. In a medium bowl, toss together cherries, granulated sugar, cornstarch, and vanilla.

2. Roll out 1 disk pâte brisée to a ⅛-inch thickness on a lightly floured surface. Fit dough into a 9-inch pie plate. Pour in filling and dot with butter. Transfer to refrigerator to chill while making top crust.

3. Roll remaining disk pâte brisée to a ⅛-inch thickness on a lightly floured surface. Using a pastry wheel or sharp knife, cut 15 strips of dough: four 1-inch wide, five ½-inch wide, and six ¼-inch wide. Holding strips at each end, gently twist and then place on a parchment-lined baking sheet; chill until firm, about 10 minutes. Lay strips across pie in desired order. Trim crusts to a 1-inch overhang, using kitchen shears, and press together to seal around edges. Freeze for 20 minutes.

4. In a small bowl, whisk egg with heavy cream. Brush crust with egg wash and sprinkle with sanding sugar. Bake pie on a foil-lined rimmed baking sheet set on the middle rack, until pie is bubbling in center and crust is golden, 1 hour 30 minutes to 1 hour 45 minutes. (If crust is browning too quickly, tent with foil during last 15 minutes.) Transfer pie to a wire rack to cool before serving with whipped cream.

MELON POPS

Three kinds of melon give these artful ice pops a tie-dyed look. Cantaloupe, honeydew, and watermelon are blended individually with lime juice and condensed milk (or coconut condensed milk for a vegan version), then frozen in molds. For quicker pops, go with just one or two flavors (see Tip, below). **SERVES 10**

1½ cups each watermelon, cantaloupe, and honeydew cubes (keep fruits separate)

6 tablespoons sweetened condensed milk or coconut condensed milk, plus more as needed

6 tablespoons fresh lime juice (from 2 limes)

Kosher salt

1. Purée watermelon, 2 tablespoons condensed milk, 2 tablespoons lime juice, and a pinch of salt in a blender until smooth. Taste for sweetness; add more condensed milk as desired. Transfer to a pourable container. Rinse blender; repeat with cantaloupe and honeydew.

2. Pour 1 to 2 tablespoons of one fruit purée into each pop mold. Add 1 to 2 tablespoons each of other two fruit purées and repeat process until molds are filled to within ¼ inch from top. Freeze until firm, at least 8 hours or up to 1 month. To serve, run molds under warm water for a few seconds to release and unmold.

TIP:
For single-flavor pops, use 4½ cups of one melon variety. For two-flavor, use 2¼ cups each of different melons; purée each with half the condensed milk and lime juice and a pinch of salt.

NECTARINE AND ALMOND TART

This dessert tastes like something a French pastry chef might whip up, but it's easy to put together. Store-bought puff pastry forms the delicate golden base, and a food processor makes quick work of the almond filling. Sliced nectarines are a natural match with almonds, but peaches would also do. **SERVES 24**

½ cup blanched almonds (2 ounces)

¼ cup sugar

2 tablespoons unbleached all-purpose flour, plus more for dusting

3 tablespoons unsalted butter, room temperature

1 large egg, lightly beaten

½ teaspoon vanilla extract

1 package (14 ounces) all-butter puff pastry, such as Dufour, thawed if frozen

2 yellow nectarines, halved, pitted, and cut into ¼-inch slices (keep slices together; about 10 ounces)

¼ cup apricot preserves

1. Preheat oven to 400°F. Pulse almonds, sugar, and flour in a food processor until finely ground. With an electric mixer on medium-high, beat butter in a medium bowl until pale and fluffy, about 3 minutes. Beat in egg and vanilla, then almond mixture.

2. On a lightly floured surface, roll out puff pastry to a 9-inch square. With a small offset spatula, spread almond-butter mixture on pastry, leaving a ½-inch border. Shingle nectarines over almond-butter mixture.

3. Bake until pastry is golden and puffed and fruit is tender (if bubbles form in pastry, pierce with a knife to deflate), about 35 minutes.

4. In a small saucepan over medium-low, heat apricot preserves until warmed through, stirring occasionally. Strain through a fine-mesh sieve; discard solids. Brush fruit with preserves. Transfer to a wire rack to cool 20 minutes before slicing and serving.

BLACKBERRY PIE

Have you ever thought of enhancing fresh, juicy blackberries with a hint of oregano? You could leave it out—the dessert will be delicious anyway— but the flavor is truly next level. We topped this pie with overlapping disks of dough, shaped with a one-inch fluted cookie cutter, allowing just enough bubbling goodness to peek through. **SERVES 8**

FOR THE CRUST

4 cups plus
2 tablespoons unbleached
all-purpose flour,
plus more for dusting

2 teaspoons kosher salt

3 sticks (1½ cups)
cold unsalted butter,
cut into small pieces

½ cup to ¾ cup
ice-cold water

FOR THE FILLING

7 cups blackberries
(about 2 pounds)

1 tablespoon
fresh lemon juice

¾ cup granulated sugar

1 tablespoon finely
chopped fresh oregano
(optional)

¼ cup cornstarch

Pinch of kosher salt

1 large egg, lightly beaten,
for egg wash

Coarse sanding sugar,
for sprinkling

Whipped Cream
(page 246), for serving

1. Make the crust: Pulse flour and salt in a food processor until combined. Add butter and pulse just until mixture resembles coarse meal, with a few pea-size pieces of butter remaining, about 10 seconds. Drizzle in ½ cup ice water, pulsing until dough just holds together, about 30 seconds. Test dough at this point by squeezing a small amount together. If it is too dry, drizzle in up to ¼ cup more ice water. Divide dough into thirds, pat each into a disk, and wrap in plastic. Refrigerate until firm, at least 1 hour or up to 2 days.

2. On a lightly floured piece of parchment, roll out 1 disk of dough to an 11-inch round, about ¼ inch thick. Fit into a 9-inch pie plate. Trim overhang to just beyond rim of pie plate; tuck under to create a neat edge all around. Refrigerate until firm, about 30 minutes. Roll out remaining 2 disks of dough to just under ¼ inch thick. Transfer dough on parchment to a rimmed baking sheet and freeze until firm, about 30 minutes. Using a 1-inch fluted cookie cutter, cut out as many rounds as possible from dough (we cut out about 100), rerolling the scraps and cutting out more rounds. Return cutouts to freezer while you make filling.

3. Make the filling: In a large bowl, toss berries with lemon juice, granulated sugar, oregano (if using), cornstarch, and salt. Transfer fruit to piecrust. Brush edge of piecrust with beaten egg and arrange overlapping rounds of dough on top of edge. Continue overlapping rounds to cover pie. Freeze pie until firm, about 1 hour.

4. Preheat oven to 400°F with a rack in lower third and a foil-lined baking sheet on rack below. Brush entire top of pie with egg wash and sprinkle with sanding sugar. Bake 30 minutes. Reduce heat to 375°F and continue to bake until juices are bubbling (if browning too quickly, tent with foil), about 1 hour more. Let cool completely, at least 6 hours or overnight. Serve with whipped cream.

MIXED-BERRY GRUNT

One of a slew of classic fruit desserts with funny names (hello, fools, buckles, and pandowdies), the grunt, some say, earned its title from the dumplings that simmer—a bit noisily—in the filling on the stove. Or maybe it comes from the satisfied sound you make after your first, cream-drizzled spoonful? Whatever it is, it's darn good. **SERVES 8**

1 cup sugar

¼ teaspoon plus a pinch of ground cinnamon

¾ cup unbleached all-purpose flour

¾ teaspoon baking powder

Kosher salt

¼ teaspoon ground ginger

⅓ cup whole milk, room temperature

2 tablespoons unsalted butter, melted

1 pound fresh raspberries (about 4 cups)

1 pound fresh blackberries (about 3 cups)

2 tablespoons fresh lemon juice

Heavy cream, for drizzling

1. In a small bowl, stir together 2 tablespoons sugar and ¼ teaspoon cinnamon. In a medium bowl, whisk together flour, 2 tablespoons sugar, the baking powder, a pinch of salt, and the ginger. In a small bowl, stir together milk and butter. Stir milk-butter mixture into flour mixture until combined; set batter aside.

2. In a large straight-sided skillet (off heat), gently fold together raspberries, blackberries, lemon juice, remaining ¾ cup sugar, a pinch of salt, the remaining pinch of cinnamon, and 2 tablespoons water. Cover and bring to a boil over medium-high heat, stirring occasionally.

3. Using two spoons, drop 8 large dollops of batter on top of berry mixture, spacing them evenly. Sprinkle dumplings with cinnamon-sugar mixture. Cover and reduce heat to medium. Cook until dumplings are set, tops are dry, and juices are bubbling, about 15 minutes. Serve warm, drizzled with cream.

MINI PEACH-APRICOT COBBLERS

Ripe stone fruit, tender biscuit dough (see Tip), and a filling redolent with cardamom and allspice make these personal-size cobblers scrumptious. If you prefer one large cobbler, use a 2½-quart dish and bake 1 hour 15 minutes. Serving with ice cream is optional, but who are we kidding? **SERVES 6**

FOR THE FILLING

6 peaches, halved, pitted, and cut into ½-inch-thick wedges

4 to 5 apricots, halved, pitted, and cut into ½-inch-thick wedges

⅔ cup granulated sugar

3 tablespoons cornstarch

1 tablespoon lemon juice

¼ teaspoon ground cardamom

¼ teaspoon ground allspice

½ teaspoon kosher salt

FOR THE BISCUITS

1½ cups unbleached all-purpose flour

3 tablespoons granulated sugar

1½ teaspoons baking powder

¼ teaspoon baking soda

¾ teaspoon kosher salt

6 tablespoons cold unsalted butter, cut into pieces

⅓ cup buttermilk

⅓ cup heavy cream, plus more for brushing

Fine sanding sugar, for sprinkling

1. Make the filling: Preheat oven to 375°F. In a large bowl, stir together peaches, apricots, granulated sugar, cornstarch, lemon juice, cardamom, allspice, and salt. Divide mixture among six 1½-cup ramekins or gratin dishes (about 1⅓ cups each).

2. Make the biscuits: In a medium bowl, whisk together flour, granulated sugar, baking powder, baking soda, and salt. Cut in butter with a pastry blender, or rub in with your fingers, until mixture resembles coarse meal with some pea-size pieces of butter remaining. With a wooden spoon, stir in buttermilk and cream until a soft, sticky dough forms.

3. Spoon about ⅓ cup dough on top of each ramekin (fruit mixture should not be completely covered). Brush tops with cream and sprinkle with sanding sugar. Transfer to a baking sheet and bake until golden brown and bubbling, 55 to 70 minutes. Let cool 30 minutes before serving.

TIP:
When combining butter and dry biscuit ingredients, leave small pieces (if using fingers, stop when the butter is at the "flower petal" stage) to melt in the oven. That creates steam and helps the dough rise.

JAM CRUMB CAKE

You'll want to set aside extra jam this season for baking this scrumptious snacking cake. Jam freezes beautifully, so it's easy to make some extra now and enjoy the taste of summer all year long. We used plum here, but you can substitute any flavor you have—and get ready to share. **SERVES 12 TO 16**

FOR THE TOPPING

1 cup unbleached
all-purpose flour

⅓ cup packed
light-brown sugar

¼ teaspoon kosher salt

6 tablespoons unsalted
butter, melted

FOR THE CAKE

1½ sticks (¾ cup)
unsalted butter,
room temperature,
plus more for pan

2 cups unbleached
all-purpose flour

2 teaspoons
baking powder

¾ teaspoon kosher salt

¾ cup granulated sugar

2 large eggs, room
temperature

⅔ cup whole milk,
room temperature

1½ cups Summer Jam
(page 240)

1. Make the topping: In a small bowl, whisk together flour, brown sugar, and salt. Stir in melted butter until combined.

2. Make the cake: Preheat oven to 350°F. Brush a 9-by-9-by- 2-inch square cake pan (not nonstick) with butter. Line with parchment, leaving a 2-inch overhang on two sides; butter parchment.

3. In a medium bowl, whisk together flour, baking powder, and salt. In another bowl, with an electric mixer on medium-high speed, beat butter with granulated sugar until light and fluffy, about 2 minutes. Add eggs, one at a time, beating to combine after each. Reduce speed to low and add flour mixture in three batches, alternating with two additions of milk, beginning and ending with the flour mixture, beating until combined and scraping down bowl as necessary.

4. Transfer batter to prepared pan. Spread jam evenly over top, using a small offset spatula. Sprinkle evenly with topping, squeezing to create large clumps. Bake until a cake tester inserted in center comes out clean, 45 to 50 minutes. Transfer pan to a wire rack to cool 20 minutes. Use parchment to lift cake out of pan, then let cool completely on rack before serving.

ALMOND PLUM CAKE

This cake puts its best face forward, thanks to vivid red (or purple) plum slices arranged whimsically on top. Almond flour doesn't just make it gluten-free; it also happens to be a match made in taste-bud heaven. **SERVES 8**

1 stick (½ cup) unsalted butter, melted and cooled slightly, plus more for pan

1⅓ cups blanched finely ground almond flour

⅔ cup fine yellow cornmeal

1 teaspoon baking powder

Pinch of kosher salt

2 large eggs, room temperature

⅔ cup plus 1 teaspoon sugar

1 teaspoon vanilla extract

Pinch of ground cinnamon

2 to 3 red or purple plums (about 6 ounces), halved, pitted, and sliced into ½-inch wedges

1. Preheat oven to 350°F. Brush an 8-inch springform pan with butter.

2. In a medium bowl, whisk together almond flour, cornmeal, baking powder, and salt.

3. With an electric mixer on medium-high speed, beat eggs and ⅔ cup sugar in a large bowl until thick and tripled in volume, about 3 minutes. Beat in melted butter and vanilla. Reduce speed to low, add flour mixture, and beat until well combined. Pour batter into prepared pan, smoothing top with an offset spatula. Arrange plums over batter.

4. In a small bowl, combine cinnamon and remaining 1 teaspoon sugar. Bake until plums are soft and a cake tester inserted into center comes out clean, 50 to 55 minutes. Transfer pan to a wire rack, sprinkle with cinnamon-sugar, and let cool 10 minutes. Run a thin metal spatula or knife around edges of pan to loosen cake. Remove outer ring from pan and cool completely on rack before serving.

TIP:
You can find almond flour, which has a finer grind than almond meal, in most large markets. Store it in the refrigerator for up to 6 months, or in the freezer for up to 12 months. To make your own, pulse blanched almonds in a food processor until finely ground.

PEACH CHIFFON PIE

On a sultry late-summer day, when you can't imagine turning on the oven and those farmers' market tables are heavy with ripe stone fruit, think peach chiffon pie. It's cool and intensely fruity, and the most difficult step is waiting for it to chill. Use that time wisely— on the porch with a good book. **SERVES 8 TO 10**

FOR THE CRUST

6 ounces gingersnap cookies (about 22)

4 tablespoons unsalted butter, melted

½ teaspoon kosher salt

FOR THE PEACH CHIFFON

1 tablespoon unflavored powdered gelatin (from two ¼-ounce envelopes)

¼ cup cold water

2 pounds peaches (7 to 8 medium), pitted and coarsely chopped, plus wedges for serving

2 tablespoons fresh lemon juice

¾ cup sugar, plus more for sprinkling basil leaves

1 sprig basil, plus 8 to 10 leaves for garnish

¾ teaspoon kosher salt

1¼ cups cold heavy cream

¾ teaspoon vanilla extract

1 large egg white

1. Make the crust: Pulse cookies in a food processor until finely ground. Add butter and salt and pulse until mixture has the texture of wet sand. Press into the bottom and up sides of a 10-inch fluted tart pan with a removable bottom or a pie dish. Freeze until firm, 30 minutes.

2. Make the peach chiffon: In a small bowl, sprinkle gelatin over cold water and let stand 5 minutes. In a large saucepan, combine peaches, lemon juice, ½ cup sugar, basil sprig, ¾ cup water, and salt. Bring to a boil, then cover, reduce heat to medium-low, and simmer until peaches are very soft, about 15 minutes. Strain through a fine-mesh sieve into a medium bowl, pressing on solids to extract as much liquid and pulp as possible; discard solids. Stir in gelatin until dissolved. Refrigerate until thickened slightly, about 1 hour, or place in a bowl set over an ice-water bath and stir occasionally, about 10 minutes.

3. Beat cream with remaining ¼ cup sugar and the vanilla just to soft peaks. Gently fold whipped cream into chilled peach purée. Pour mixture into crust and freeze until firm, at least 4 hours or up to 1 day.

4. In a small bowl, whisk egg white with 1 tablespoon water until frothy. Working with one leaf at a time, brush a thin layer of egg wash onto basil, then sprinkle with sugar. Transfer to a wire rack to cool until firm and dry, about 1 hour. (Raw eggs should not be used in food prepared for pregnant women, babies, young children, elderly, or anyone whose health is compromised.)

5. Remove pie from freezer 15 to 20 minutes before serving. Arrange peach wedges in center and scatter sugared basil leaves across pie. Cut into wedges to serve.

BERRY CORNMEAL SHEET CAKE

Though your guests are sure to welcome it on any summer day, consider whipping up this red, white, and blue beauty on the Fourth—the mixed berries and whipped cream supply that perfectly patriotic color scheme. **SERVES 12**

1½ sticks (¾ cup) unsalted butter, room temperature, plus more for pan

1½ cups unbleached all-purpose flour

¾ cup fine yellow cornmeal

1½ teaspoons baking powder

¾ teaspoon kosher salt

1½ cups plus 2 tablespoons sugar

3 large eggs, room temperature

1½ teaspoons vanilla extract

¾ cup buttermilk, room temperature

18 ounces mixed fresh berries, such as blueberries, raspberries, and blackberries (about 4 cups), plus more for serving

Whipped Cream (page 246), for serving

1. Preheat oven to 325°F. Butter a 9-by-13-inch baking pan and line with parchment, leaving overhang on both long sides. Butter parchment. In a medium bowl, whisk together flour, cornmeal, baking powder, and salt.

2. With an electric mixer on medium-high speed, beat butter and 1½ cups sugar in a large bowl until pale and fluffy, about 2 minutes. Add eggs, one at a time, beating well after each addition and scraping down sides of bowl as needed. Beat in vanilla. Add flour mixture in three batches, alternating with two batches of buttermilk, beginning and ending with flour mixture, and beating until just combined. Spread batter evenly in prepared pan, smoothing top with a small offset spatula.

3. Sprinkle berries over top, then sprinkle with remaining 2 tablespoons sugar. Bake until golden brown and a cake tester comes out clean, about 1 hour. Transfer to a wire rack to cool. Using parchment overhang, remove cake from pan to a cutting board and cut into pieces. Serve with whipped cream and additional berries.

RED AND BLACK PLUM TART

With this jewel-toned tart in your repertoire, you'll have the dream finale for brunches or backyard suppers all season. Just pick up ripe plums— a mix of red and black—at the market and pull store-bought puff pastry from the freezer. Arrange the fruit in stripes for graphic appeal. **SERVES 8**

2 tablespoons skin-on almonds, toasted (page 246)

2 tablespoons sugar

1 tablespoon unbleached all-purpose flour, plus more for dusting

1 package (14 ounces) all-butter puff pastry, such as Dufour, thawed

1 large egg yolk

1 tablespoon heavy cream

5 black plums (about 12 ounces), pitted and cut into ¼-inch slices (about 2 cups)

5 red plums (about 12 ounces), pitted and cut into ¼-inch slices (about 2 cups)

1 cup apricot jam

1. Pulse almonds, 1 tablespoon sugar, and the flour in a food processor until ground to a fine meal.

2. Roll out puff pastry into a 10-by-14-inch rectangle, about ⅛ inch thick, on a lightly floured surface. Using a paring knife, score a ½-inch border on all sides, being careful not to cut all the way through. Place pastry on a parchment-lined baking sheet and freeze until firm, about 30 minutes.

3. Preheat oven to 375°F. In a small bowl, whisk together egg yolk and cream. Brush border with egg wash, then sprinkle almond mixture evenly over center of pastry. Alternate even rows of black and red plum slices. Freeze tart until firm, about 30 minutes.

4. Sprinkle remaining tablespoon sugar over top, then bake until edges are golden brown, about 40 minutes.

5. In a small saucepan, warm apricot jam over medium-low heat. Strain through a fine-mesh sieve; discard solids. Brush plums with warm jam. Transfer to a wire rack to cool. Serve warm or at room temperature.

PEACH MELBA SPOOM

You've heard, perhaps, of the Italian ice-cream treat known as spumoni. A spoom comes from the same root word, spuma, *meaning "foam," and both rely on voluminous whipped egg whites for their light, frothy consistency. This whipped meringue dessert, though, is dairy-free. Think sorbet, only airier.* **SERVES 4**

½ cup plus ⅓ cup sugar

5 peaches
(about 1¼ pounds),
halved and pitted

12 ounces raspberries
(3 cups)

2 large egg whites,
room temperature

1. In a small saucepan, bring ½ cup sugar and ½ cup water to a boil, stirring, until sugar dissolves. Let cool slightly. Refrigerate syrup until chilled, about 30 minutes.

2. Add 3 peaches, half the raspberries, and ¼ cup syrup to a food processor and purée until smooth. Add more syrup to taste (reserve remaining syrup for another use). Strain mixture through a fine-mesh sieve over a bowl, pressing on solids to extract liquids; discard solids. Refrigerate for at least 1 hour.

3. In a heatproof bowl set over (not in) a pan of simmering water, place egg whites and remaining ⅓ cup sugar. Cook, whisking constantly, until sugar dissolves and mixture is hot to the touch, about 2 minutes. With bowl still over heat and an electric mixer on high speed, whisk until stiff, glossy peaks form, about 5 minutes.

4. Remove bowl from heat. Using a whisk, gently fold fruit purée into beaten whites. Freeze and churn mixture in an ice-cream maker according to manufacturer's directions. Transfer spoom to an airtight container and freeze for at least 1 hour.

5. Slice remaining 2 peaches and crush remaining raspberries in a small bowl. Layer fruit with spoom in 4 glasses and serve immediately.

TIP:
An ice-cream maker is a must to achieve the desired light consistency in this frozen treat.

DOUBLE-CRUST FREE-FORM BERRY PIE

When a big crowd is coming for dinner, clear off some counter space and make one giant, glorious pie. This mixed-berry delight calls for 2 large rounds of dough, a 15-inch and an 18-inch, so you'll need to double the pâte brisée recipe (page 236). For time-saving embellishment, make a "cheat" lattice using a 1-inch square cutter to form a grid in the top crust. **SERVES 14**

Unbleached all-purpose flour, for dusting

2 large disks Pâte Brisée (double the recipe on page 236)

2½ pounds mixed blackberries and raspberries (8 to 9 cups)

3 tablespoons cornstarch

½ cup granulated sugar

2 tablespoons fresh lemon juice

1 large egg, lightly beaten, for egg wash

Fine sanding sugar, for sprinkling

1. On a lightly floured piece of parchment, roll out one disk of dough to an 18-inch round. Transfer dough on parchment to a baking sheet and refrigerate until just firm, about 10 minutes. Meanwhile, on another lightly floured piece of parchment, roll out remaining disk of dough to a 15-inch round. Leaving a 1-inch border, punch out squares with a 1-inch square cutter in rows, spaced about ¾ inch apart, to form a grid. Transfer dough on parchment to another baking sheet and refrigerate 10 minutes.

2. In a medium bowl, toss berries with cornstarch, granulated sugar, and lemon juice. Spread mixture evenly over center of 18-inch dough round, leaving a 3½-inch border. Center second dough round on top of berries; brush with egg wash. Fold bottom dough over top, pressing to seal and forming pleats as you go. Brush folded edges with egg wash and sprinkle entire surface with sanding sugar. Freeze until firm, about 30 minutes.

3. Preheat oven to 375°F. Bake pie, rotating halfway through, until golden brown and juices are bubbling in center, about 1 hour 10 minutes. Let cool on a wire rack at least 1 hour before serving.

TIP:
Don't toss those pastry cutouts. Brush them with egg wash, sprinkle with cinnamon and sanding sugar, and bake about 15 minutes at 375°F. They're perfect with a cup of tea while you wait for your guests to arrive.

TRIPLE-BERRY SWIRL ICE-CREAM SANDWICHES

A homemade chocolate cookie and fresh berries put these grab-and-go treats miles above anything in the freezer section. Swirl the berry purée throughout the vanilla ice cream (churn your own if you like, or save time with store-bought) so each slice is just the right bite. **MAKES 12**

FOR THE FRUIT FILLING

½ cup raspberries
(about 2 ounces)

½ cup blackberries
(about 2 ½ ounces)

½ cup chopped
strawberries
(about 3 ounces)

⅓ cup sugar

1 tablespoon
fresh lemon juice

1 tablespoon cornstarch

Pinch of kosher salt

FOR THE COOKIES

6 tablespoons unsalted
butter, room temperature,
plus more for pan

1⅓ cups unbleached
all-purpose flour

¼ cup unsweetened
Dutch-process cocoa
powder, such as Valrhona

1 teaspoon baking powder

¼ teaspoon kosher salt

¾ cup sugar

2 teaspoons
vanilla extract

1 large egg

3 pints vanilla
ice cream, softened

1. Make the fruit filling: In a small saucepan, combine raspberries, blackberries, strawberries, sugar, lemon juice, cornstarch, and salt. Cook over medium heat, stirring, until berries start to break up and release their juices. Continue to cook, smashing berries against side of pan and stirring frequently, until fruit breaks down and juices are thickened, about 2 minutes more. Strain berry mixture through a fine-mesh sieve into a medium heatproof bowl or measuring cup (you should have about ½ cup mixture). Let cool to room temperature.

2. Make the cookies: Preheat oven to 350°F. Butter a 9-by-13-inch rimmed baking sheet pan. Line with parchment, leaving overhang on two long sides; butter parchment. In a medium bowl, whisk together flour, cocoa, baking powder, and salt. In another medium bowl, beat butter, sugar, and vanilla with an electric mixer on medium speed until light and fluffy, about 2 minutes. Add egg and beat until combined. Reduce speed to low, add flour mixture in two batches, and beat until just incorporated. Press batter evenly in prepared pan.

3. Bake until cookie is dry to the touch and edges begin to pull away from pan, 14 to 16 minutes. Transfer to a wire rack to cool. Using parchment overhang, transfer cookie to a work surface. Cut in half crosswise. Place one half, top-side up, on a piece of plastic wrap.

4. In a large bowl, beat ice cream with mixer until malleable. Pour cooled berry mixture over top, and, with a spatula, gently swirl into ice cream. (If ice cream is too soft, freeze in bowl for 30 minutes to firm up before proceeding.)

5. Spread swirled ice cream over cookie on plastic wrap, extending to edges of cookie. Top with remaining cookie, bottom-side up. Wrap in plastic and freeze at least 4 hours or up to 1 week. Use a serrated knife to trim edges and cut into twelve 1¼-by-3-inch pieces. Serve immediately or wrap tightly in plastic and freeze for up to 1 week.

PLUM TART WITH BROWN-SUGAR CRUMBLE

They say what grows together, goes together, and that can be true even of summer fruit with blooms that share its season. Take this pretty plum tart with brown-sugar crumble: A sprinkle of rose water enhances the fruit and imparts a delicate aroma that will transport you straight to the garden. **SERVES 10**

FOR THE CRUST

1¼ cups unbleached all-purpose flour, plus more for dusting

¼ cup granulated sugar

Pinch of kosher salt

1 stick (½ cup) cold unsalted butter, cut into small pieces

2 large egg yolks

1 tablespoon ice-cold water

FOR THE FILLING

2 pounds mixed plums (about 12 medium), halved and pitted

⅓ cup granulated sugar

⅓ cup packed light-brown sugar

2 tablespoons cornstarch

Pinch of kosher salt

1 teaspoon rose water (optional)

FOR THE CRUMBLE

¼ cup packed light-brown sugar

4 tablespoons unsalted butter, room temperature

½ cup unbleached all-purpose flour

¼ teaspoon kosher salt

1. Make the crust: Pulse flour, granulated sugar, and salt in a food processor. Add butter and pulse until mixture resembles coarse meal, with a few pea-size pieces of butter remaining. Add egg yolks and ice water and pulse just until dough comes together. Pat into a disk, wrap in plastic, and refrigerate at least 1 hour or up to overnight.

2. Roll out dough to a roughly 13-inch round, about ¼ inch thick, on a lightly floured surface. Fit into an 11-inch fluted tart pan with a removable bottom. Trim edge of dough flush with top of pan. Freeze until firm, about 1 hour.

3. Make the filling: Preheat oven to 400°F with a rack in lower third. In a medium bowl, toss plums, granulated and brown sugars, cornstarch, salt, and rose water, if desired, to combine. Spread in tart shell in a single layer.

4. Make the crumble: In a small bowl, combine brown sugar, butter, flour, and salt and mix with fingertips until clumps form. Crumble evenly over filling.

5. Bake on a rimmed baking sheet until juices are bubbling and topping is browned, about 50 minutes. Transfer to a wire rack to cool completely. (Tart is best served the day it's made.)

DOUBLE-CRUST PEACH SLAB PIE

Picnic season and peach season collide in the ultimate sheet-pan dessert– the slab pie. It's lush with peaches and can feed a crowd as well as two 9-inch round pies can, but it's quicker to assemble (we use a jelly-roll pan) and easier to slice into small portions. **SERVES 12 TO 16**

5 cups unbleached all-purpose flour, plus more for dusting

1¼ teaspoons kosher salt

¾ cup plus 2 tablespoons sugar

4 sticks (2 cups) cold unsalted butter, cut into small pieces

⅔ cup ice-cold water, plus up to ½ cup more

3¾ pounds peaches, pitted and thinly sliced (12 cups)

¼ cup cornstarch

1 tablespoon finely grated lemon zest plus 2 tablespoons fresh lemon juice

1. Pulse flour, salt, and 2 tablespoons sugar in a food processor until combined. Add butter and pulse until mixture resembles coarse meal, with a few pea-size pieces of butter remaining. With machine running, add ⅔ cup ice water until just incorporated. Squeeze a small amount of dough to make sure it holds together (if necessary, add up to ½ cup more ice water, 1 tablespoon at a time). Do not overmix. Divide dough in half, gather into 2 flat rectangles, and wrap each in plastic. Refrigerate until firm, at least 1 hour or up to overnight.

2. Preheat oven to 400°F. In a large bowl, toss together peaches, remaining ¾ cup sugar, the cornstarch, and lemon zest and juice.

3. Lightly flour a work surface and rolling pin. Roll out 1 piece of dough into a 12-by-16-inch rectangle. Roll dough over rolling pin; carefully unroll into a 10½-by-15¼-inch jelly-roll pan. Press gently to fit into pan.

4. Pour in peach filling, then lightly brush edges of dough with water. On floured surface, roll out remaining dough into an 11-by-15-inch rectangle. Roll dough over rolling pin and carefully unroll over filling. Press along moistened edges to seal. Fold under any overhang, tucking it into pan. With your fingers, crimp edges.

5. With a paring knife, cut slits on top to vent. Place pie in oven, then reduce heat to 375°F. Bake until crust is golden and juices are bubbling, 45 to 50 minutes. Transfer to a wire rack to cool 1 hour. Serve warm or at room temperature.

MIXED-BERRY GALETTE

Piles of ripe berries are paired with a creamy almond filling in this oval tart, in which you simply fold over and pleat the edges of the pastry to form the border around the fruit. The almond frangipane mixes up quickly and can be made a day ahead. **SERVES 8**

FOR THE FRANGIPANE

⅓ cup blanched almonds

¼ cup sugar

3 tablespoons unsalted butter, room temperature

1 tablespoon unbleached all-purpose flour

1 large egg, separated (reserve egg white for crust)

1 tablespoon rum

½ teaspoon kosher salt

FOR THE CRUST AND FILLING

2 tablespoons unbleached all-purpose flour, plus more for dusting

1 disk Pâte Brisée (page 236)

12 ounces mixed berries, such as blueberries, raspberries, blackberries, and sliced strawberries (about 2½ cups)

⅓ cup sugar

1 teaspoon fresh lemon juice

¼ teaspoon kosher salt

Whipped Cream (page 246), for serving

1. Make the frangipane: Preheat oven to 375°F. Toast almonds on a baking sheet, stirring once, until deep golden brown, about 12 minutes. Let cool completely, about 15 minutes. Pulse in a food processor until finely ground. Add sugar, butter, flour, egg yolk, rum, and salt and process until smooth. (Frangipane can be made in advance, and stored in an airtight container in refrigerator up to 1 day; return to room temperature before using.)

2. Make the crust and filling: On lightly floured parchment, roll pâte brisée dough into an oval, about ⅛ inch thick. Transfer on parchment to a rimmed baking sheet. Spread frangipane evenly over dough, leaving a 2-inch border. In a medium bowl, stir together berries, sugar, flour, lemon juice, and salt. Arrange fruit mixture in a single layer over frangipane. Fold dough over fruit, leaving center uncovered. In a small bowl, lightly beat egg white. Brush crust with egg wash, brushing under folds to help seal.

3. Bake until golden brown and bubbling in center, 50 minutes to 1 hour. Transfer galette on parchment to a wire rack to cool slightly. Serve warm or at room temperature with whipped cream. (The galette is best eaten the day it's made but can be stored, lightly tented with foil, for up to 1 day at room temperature.)

MINI APRICOT TARTES TATIN

A standard muffin tin is practically all the equipment you need to make miniature versions of this classic bistro dessert. Butter the pan, then layer in a few basic ingredients: caramel, halved apricots, then rounds of pâte brisée. Invert the tin after baking to reveal sublime single servings. **SERVES 12**

4 tablespoons unsalted butter, room temperature, plus more for pan

Unbleached all-purpose flour, for dusting

1 disk Pâte Brisée (page 236)

½ cup sugar

12 firm but ripe apricots, halved and pitted

Whipped Cream (page 246), for serving (optional)

1. Preheat oven to 425°F with a rack in upper third. Line a rimmed baking sheet with parchment. Generously butter a standard 12-cup nonstick muffin pan. On a lightly floured surface, roll out pâte brisée to about ⅛-inch thickness. Using a 3-inch round cookie cutter, cut out 12 rounds. Transfer rounds to prepared baking sheet and place in freezer for 15 to 20 minutes.

2. In a small heavy saucepan over medium-high heat, combine sugar with 3 tablespoons water, swirling pan occasionally (do not stir), until deep amber, about 8 minutes. Remove from heat and whisk in butter. Divide caramel evenly among prepared muffin cups. Place 2 apricot halves, cut-side up, in each muffin cup. Remove chilled pastry rounds from freezer and place on top of apricots.

3. Place muffin pan on chilled baking sheet and bake, rotating pan halfway through, until pastry is crisp and golden brown, 30 to 32 minutes. Transfer to a wire rack to cool. Top muffin pan with a rimmed baking sheet and invert. Transfer to a wire rack to cool. Serve with whipped cream, if desired.

HUCKLEBERRY COBBLER

The humble huckleberry—tart, sweet, and bursting with finger-staining dark red juice—shows up this time of year in farmers' markets and growing in the wild. If you find some, show them off in this rustic, cornmeal-fortified cake. If the bears get them first, wild blueberries make a fine swap. **SERVES 8**

1 stick (1/2 cup)
unsalted butter

3 cups huckleberries

1 cup plus
2 tablespoons sugar

1 cup unbleached
all-purpose flour

1/4 cup cornmeal

1 teaspoon baking powder

1/2 teaspoon kosher salt

1 cup whole milk

1 vanilla bean, split
and seeds scraped, or
1 teaspoon vanilla extract

1. Preheat oven to 350°F. Melt butter in a 10-inch cast-iron skillet in oven, about 5 minutes.

2. In a medium bowl, toss huckleberries with 2 tablespoons sugar. In a large bowl, whisk together flour, cornmeal, baking powder, salt, and remaining 1 cup sugar. Add milk and vanilla seeds. Remove skillet from oven and add melted butter to flour mixture; whisk until just combined. Pour batter into skillet and top with huckleberries and the juices.

3. Bake until golden brown and fruit is bubbling, 40 to 45 minutes. Let stand 10 minutes before serving.

TIP:
A cast-iron skillet
is a charming
delivery system for this
dessert, but if you
don't have one, use a
10-inch pie dish.

NECTARINE AND RASPBERRY CRISP

This almost effortless crisp is more than the sum of its parts. Toss sweet-tangy fruit in a dish, stir together a quick topping—cornmeal takes the place of the usual oats in this one for satisfying crunch— then bake to bubbling perfection. **SERVES 8**

FOR THE FILLING

1½ pounds nectarines (about 5), pitted and cut into ½-inch wedges

6 ounces raspberries (1⅓ cups)

⅔ cup granulated sugar

1 tablespoon cornstarch

¼ teaspoon kosher salt

FOR THE TOPPING

1 stick unsalted butter, room temperature

½ cup packed light-brown sugar

¾ cup unbleached all-purpose flour

½ cup fine yellow cornmeal

½ teaspoon kosher salt

1. Make the filling: Preheat oven to 375°F. In a medium bowl, combine nectarines, raspberries, granulated sugar, cornstarch, and salt. Transfer to 9-inch square baking pan.

2. Make the topping: In a large bowl, beat butter and brown sugar with an electric mixer on medium speed until light and fluffy. With your fingertips, work flour, cornmeal, and salt into butter mixture until large clumps form. Scatter over filling. Bake until center is bubbling, 40 to 50 minutes. Transfer to a wire rack to let crisp cool slightly before serving.

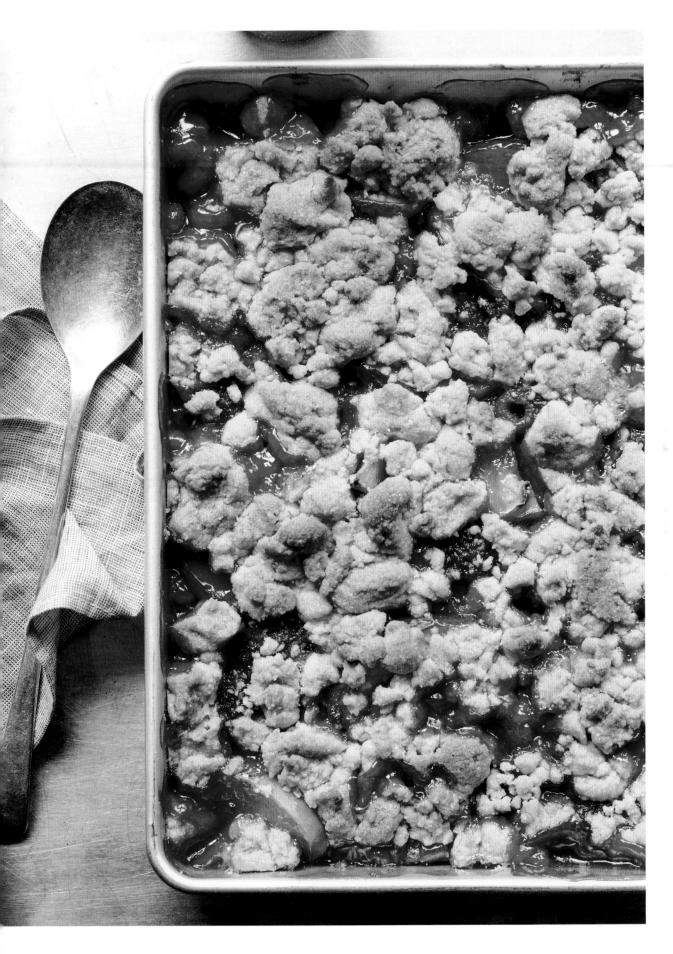

TIP:
If you don't have
Greek yogurt, put 2 cups
of regular whole-milk
yogurt in a cheesecloth-
lined colander over
a bowl and let it drain
for 2 hours in the
refrigerator. The volume
should reduce to 1 cup.

FRUIT FOOLS

A traditional English fool features custard, whipped cream, and fruit, all layered and swirled to be eaten like a parfait. Here, we simplified it for an everyday dessert and also created a healthier version, using rich Greek yogurt and honey-sweetened blueberries.

BLUEBERRY YOGURT FOOL

SERVES 4

3 cups blueberries, plus more for serving

1/3 cup honey, plus more if desired

Juice of 1/2 lime

5 fresh mint leaves

1/2 cup cold heavy cream

1 cup Greek yogurt

1. In a blender, combine blueberries, honey, lime juice, and mint leaves and purée until smooth. Strain mixture through a fine-mesh sieve into a container, pressing on solids to extract liquids; discard solids. Taste and add more honey, if desired. Cover with plastic wrap and refrigerate until cold, about 10 minutes.

2. In a medium bowl, whip cream with an electric mixer on high speed until stiff peaks form, about 3 minutes. In a separate bowl, fold cream into yogurt. In 4 glasses, alternate layers of purée and whipped cream–yogurt. With a wooden skewer or thin-bladed knife, gently swirl purée into whipped yogurt-cream, creating streaks. Garnish with berries and serve immediately or chill until ready to serve.

BLACKBERRY OR RASPBERRY FOOL

SERVES 6

3 cups blackberries or raspberries, plus more for serving

1/4 cup granulated sugar

Pinch of kosher salt

2 1/2 cups cold heavy cream

1/3 cup confectioners' sugar

4 teaspoons fresh lemon juice

1. In a blender, combine berries, granulated sugar, and salt and purée until sugar dissolves, about 1 minute. Strain mixture through a fine-mesh sieve into a medium bowl, pressing on solids to extract liquids; discard solids.

2. In a large bowl, beat cream and confectioners' sugar with an electric mixer on high speed until stiff peaks form, about 3 minutes. Beat in lemon juice. In 6 small glasses, alternate layers of berry purée and whipped cream. With a wooden skewer or thin-bladed knife, gently swirl purée into whipped cream, creating streaks. Garnish with berries and serve immediately or chill until ready to serve.

BASICS

With fruit in season, a just-right dessert is always close at hand. To put it together, all you need is a well-stocked pantry (think best-quality chocolate, vanilla, and nuts) and some essential baker's techniques.

PÂTE BRISÉE

Over the years, we have come to rely on pâte brisée for making a perfect pie dough from scratch. Butter plays a key role in helping to create that much sought-after texture—you want just the right proportion of butter to flour. This recipe yields two disks of dough, so if you're making a galette or a tart, save the second disk for another time (it freezes well for up to 3 months). Using this recipe, cold ingredients, and a light hand, you'll master the piecrust in no time.

MAKES ONE 9-INCH DOUBLE-CRUST PIE, 2 GALETTES OR TARTS, OR ONE 10½-BY-15¼-INCH SINGLE-CRUST SLAB PIE

2½ cups unbleached all-purpose flour

1 tablespoon sugar

1½ teaspoons kosher salt

2 sticks (1 cup) cold unsalted butter, cut into pieces

¼ to ½ cup ice-cold water

1. If making in a food processor: Pulse flour, sugar, and salt in a food processor until combined. Add butter and pulse until mixture resembles coarse meal, with a few pea-size pieces remaining. Drizzle with ¼ cup ice water and pulse until just incorporated. (Squeeze a small amount of dough to make sure it holds together. If dough is too dry, add up to ¼ cup more ice-cold water, 1 tablespoon at a time.) Do not overprocess; it should look like moist gravel, not a solid mass.

2. If making by hand: In a large bowl, whisk together flour, sugar, and salt. Using your fingers or a pastry cutter, work butter into mixture until it resembles coarse meal with a few flat, petal-shaped pieces of butter remaining. Drizzle with ¼ cup ice water over dough. Using a fork, mix until dough holds together when squeezed, adding up to ¼ cup more ice-cold water, 1 tablespoon at a time, if necessary. Turn out onto work surface and knead to bring dough together.

3. For a 9-inch pie or galette, shape dough into 2 disks and wrap each in plastic. For a slab pie, shape dough into a rectangle and wrap in plastic. Refrigerate until firm, at least 1 hour or up to 2 days. Dough can also be frozen up to 3 months; thaw in refrigerator before using.

TIP:
Piecrust Upgrades *(counterclockwise from bottom):* pinch to crimp; cut tabs and alternate forward; mark twice with an inverted spoon; cut out leaf shapes and adhere with egg wash; pinch to crimp then mark with fork tines.

HOW TO MAKE A SINGLE-CRUST PÂTE BRISÉE

1. Combine ingredients: Chill ingredients for 30 minutes and cut butter into cubes before combining. In a food processor, pulse just until the mixture resembles coarse meal with some pea-size pieces.

2. Drizzle in ice-cold water: Begin with ¼ cup ice water, then pulse a few times. Test the dough by squeezing it; it should be like moist gravel. Drizzle up to ¼ cup more water, as needed, 1 tablespoon at a time.

5. Roll and turn: On a lightly floured surface, roll out dough to specified dimensions. Work from the center outward, rotating dough one-eighth of a turn with every roll.

6. Transfer dough to a pie plate: Roll dough over the pin and unfurl it onto pie plate. Gently press to fit into plate. Use pastry scissors to trim excess dough to 1-inch overhang.

3. Turn dough out onto plastic wrap: With edges of plastic, gather dough up into a ball. The plastic wrap compresses ingredients while protecting them from warming under your hands.

4. Roll dough into rounds: Before chilling for 1 hour and up to 2 days, roll dough into a round approximately ½ inch thick. It will soften more uniformly when you remove it from refrigerator.

7. Crimp crust: For a classic crimp, push down and outward with your knuckle (or index finger) of one hand, while pinching with your thumb and forefinger of other hand to create a V–shape.

8. Dock crust and blind-bake: Pierce crust with a fork, preventing it from puffing up as it bakes. Chill, then line with parchment and fill with beans or pie weights. Bake just until edges begin to brown.

COOKING FRUIT

Preserving, roasting, broiling, poaching. Whether you have extra bounty from the farm stand or want to extend fruits' peak season, the techniques on the following pages will get you started.

ORANGE MARMALADE

MAKES 5 CUPS

Marmalade is a preserve made from citrus that utilizes the whole fruit, including the rind. Oranges, especially Seville, grapefruits, and lemons, notably Meyer, make lovely marmalades.

3 pounds navel oranges (about 7),
washed, ends trimmed,
and cut crosswise into thin slices

4 cups sugar

Place a small plate in freezer. In a large pot, bring oranges and 6 cups water to a boil over high heat. Reduce heat to medium and cook at a rapid simmer until oranges are tender, about 20 minutes. Add sugar, increase heat to medium–high, and stir until sugar dissolves. Return to a boil and cook, stirring often, until mixture is thick and darkens slightly, 50 to 60 minutes. (To test for doneness, drop a spoonful on the frozen plate and freeze 2 minutes. It should have a slight film that wrinkles when pushed with a finger. If it spreads out and thins, continue cooking.) Transfer marmalade to airtight containers, cover, and cool completely. (To store, refrigerate up to 1 month or freeze up to 6 months.)

SUMMER JAM

MAKES 3 CUPS

Unlike jelly, jam contains pieces of fruit. It's essentially the fruit cooked down with sugar until thick and spreadable. A little acid, often from a lemon, balances it out. You can substitute any chopped stone fruit (or berries, such as raspberries) for the plums. While plums don't need to be peeled (just lift the skins out of the cooked jam with a fork), peeling peaches and nectarines yields a smoother texture: Carve an X in the bottom of each and plunge them into boiling water for 30 seconds, then transfer them to an ice-water bath to stop the cooking; the skins will slip off.

3 pounds plums, pitted and chopped

3⅓ cups sugar

¼ teaspoon kosher salt

2 tablespoons fresh lemon juice

In a large heavy-bottomed pot, stir together plums, sugar, and salt. Bring to a boil, mashing fruit with a potato masher and stirring until sugar dissolves and mixture boils. Add lemon juice and continue to boil, stirring frequently, until bubbles slow and mixture clings to a spoon but falls off in clumps, 10 to 12 minutes. (If desired, lift out skins.) Skim foam from top. Ladle jam into clean airtight containers, leaving ¾ inch of headroom. Let cool completely. Cover, label, and refrigerate up to 1 month or freeze up to 1 year.

TIP:
To make raspberry jam, substitute 3 pounds raspberries for the plums in Summer Jam (page 240).

MARTHA'S PINK APPLESAUCE

MAKES 6 CUPS

4 pounds McIntosh apples
(12 to 13 medium), quartered and cored

2 pounds red apples (6 to 7 medium), such as
Empire or Cortland, quartered and cored

¼ cup fresh lemon juice (from 2 lemons)

1. Combine apples, lemon juice, and 1½ cups water
in a large pot. Cover and bring to a boil over high
heat, stirring occasionally. Reduce heat to medium,
partially cover, and cook, stirring occasionally,
until apples are completely soft, about 40 minutes.

2. Pass apples through a medium-mesh sieve or
a food mill fitted with the fine disk to remove
skins. Applesauce can be stored in an airtight container in refrigerator up to 1 week or in freezer up
to 3 months.

ROASTED PINEAPPLE

SERVES 4 TO 6

1 medium pineapple

⅓ cup sugar

¼ teaspoon kosher salt

2 tablespoons unsalted butter

1. Preheat oven to 450°F. Trim pineapple: Cut off
top and bottom ends. Stand on end and, with
downward strokes, cut skin off in wide strips,
removing the "eyes." Cut in half lengthwise; then
cut lengthwise into 1-inch-wide spears. Cut out
cores and discard.

2. In a small bowl, mix together sugar and salt.
Sprinkle evenly over both sides of pineapple.
Arrange in a single layer on a rimmed baking sheet.
Dot evenly with butter. Roast, turning over twice
during cooking and brushing with pan juices, until
fruit is soft and browned in spots, about 45 minutes.
Serve warm or at room temperature.

VANILLA-BEAN BAKED APPLES

SERVES 4

4 medium, thick-skinned, mildly
sweet apples, such as Rome, Macoun,
or Northern Spy (about 1½ pounds)

3 tablespoons packed
dark-brown sugar

2 tablespoons unsalted butter,
room temperature, or coconut oil

2 tablespoons finely chopped pecans or walnuts,
toasted (page 246), plus more for sprinkling

½ large vanilla bean,
split and seeds scraped

Pinch of kosher salt

Greek yogurt or vanilla ice cream,
for serving

1. Preheat oven to 375°F. Using an apple corer, core
apples three-quarters of the way down. Fit snugly
in an ovenproof skillet or a loaf pan.

2. In a small bowl, stir together brown sugar, butter,
nuts, vanilla seeds, and salt. Divide sugar mixture
among apples (about 2 teaspoons each). Sprinkle
with additional nuts. Bake until apples are soft,
about 1 hour. Serve warm with pan syrup spooned
on top and yogurt or ice cream on the side.

RHUBARB COMPOTE

MAKES 4 CUPS

Serve this over ice cream, yogurt, or pound cake or fold it into parfaits or fools.

1¾ pounds rhubarb,
ends trimmed, cut crosswise into
¾-inch pieces (about 6 cups)

1 cup sugar

2 cups halved strawberries

1 piece (1 inch) peeled
fresh ginger, finely grated

1. In a large saucepan (off heat), stir together rhubarb and sugar; let stand until rhubarb releases some liquid, about 10 minutes.

2. Bring rhubarb mixture to a boil over medium-high heat, stirring occasionally. Reduce heat; simmer, stirring occasionally, until rhubarb breaks down but some whole pieces remain, about 5 minutes. Remove from heat. Add in strawberries.

3. Place ginger in a fine-mesh sieve set over a small bowl, pressing down with the back of a spoon to extract juices (you should have about 1 teaspoon); discard solids. Stir ginger juice into rhubarb mixture. (Store rhubarb compote, in an airtight container, in the refrigerator up to 5 days.)

BROILED APRICOTS WITH GINGER WHIPPED CREAM

SERVES 4

1 piece (1 inch) peeled fresh ginger, finely grated

½ cup cold heavy cream

1 tablespoon granulated sugar

8 apricots (about 1 pound), halved and pitted

1 tablespoon unsalted butter, room temperature

4 teaspoons light-brown sugar

Pinch of ground cardamom

1. Preheat broiler to high with rack set 4 inches from heat. Place ginger in a fine-mesh sieve set over a medium bowl, pressing down with the back of a spoon to extract juices (you should have about 1 teaspoon); discard solids. Add cream and granulated sugar. With an electric mixer on medium speed, whisk until soft peaks form; refrigerate to chill.

2. Place apricots, cut-side up, on a rimmed baking sheet. In a small bowl, combine butter, brown sugar, and cardamom. Sprinkle mixture evenly over apricots. Broil until apricots just begin to char, 2 to 5 minutes. Top apricots with whipped cream and serve immediately.

HOW TO POACH FRUIT

1. Choose your fruit: Good fruit for poaching includes pears, quince, figs, pineapple, and stone fruit such as peaches, nectarines, apricots, plums, and cherries. Prep the fruit as directed.

2. Make a simple syrup: Bring equal parts water and granulated sugar to a boil. The simple syrup adds flavor and helps support the structure of the fruit as it cooks.

5. Cover with parchment: Cut a circle of parchment and cover the fruit, pressing it directly on the surface. Cook until the fruit is tender when pierced with a paring knife, 20 to 30 minutes.

6. Reduce the syrup: Transfer fruit to a heatproof bowl. Bring liquid to a boil; cook until syrupy and reduced. Discard flavorings. Pour liquid over pears; chill at least 30 minutes or overnight.

3. Add the flavorings: Here, the flavor comes from citrus, vanilla seed and pod, and star anise. Once you master the basics, play with flavors, like cardamom pods and ginger, to see what you like.

4. Add the fruit: Bring the poaching syrup to a boil. Reduce to a simmer and add the pears. The fruit needs to be submerged to be properly poached.

EXTRAS & TECHNIQUES

WHIPPED CREAM

MAKES ABOUT 2 CUPS

1 cup cold heavy cream

2 tablespoons confectioners' sugar

In a chilled medium bowl, whisk cream with an electric mixer on low speed until soft peaks form, about 3 minutes. Increase speed to medium-high, add confectioners' sugar, and whisk until stiff peaks form, about 2 more minutes. (To make maple whipped cream, substitute confectioners' sugar with ¼ cup pure maple syrup.)

KEY LIME GLAZE

MAKES ABOUT ¾ CUP

1½ cups confectioners' sugar, sifted

1 teaspoon Key lime zest plus 2 to 3 tablespoons juice (from about 4 Key limes)

In a small bowl, whisk together confectioners' sugar, 2 tablespoons lime juice, and the zest. Add up to 1 tablespoon more lime juice to achieve a honey-like consistency.

CANDIED LEMON ZEST

SERVES 8

4 medium lemons, preferably organic, well scrubbed

2 cups sugar

1 cup cool water

1. Using a vegetable peeler, remove zest from lemons, keeping pieces long. Remove white pith from zest with a paring knife. Using a very sharp knife, cut zest into a fine julienne. Transfer to a bowl and cover with boiling water. Let stand 30 minutes; drain.

2. In a small saucepan, bring sugar and cool water to a boil over medium-high heat, stirring occasionally, until sugar dissolves. Add julienned zest, reduce heat to medium-low, and cook 10 minutes. Remove from heat, cover, and let stand overnight.

SEGMENTING CITRUS

Trim the ends and set citrus flat on a work surface. Use a paring knife to cut peel and pith away from citrus, following the curve of the fruit. Working over a bowl, cut between the membranes, allowing the segments to fall into bowl. Discard membranes.

FREEZING FRUIT

Wash ripe, unbruised fruit. Allow the fruit to dry thoroughly to avoid freezer burn. Then arrange on a parchment-lined baking sheet in a single layer; don't overcrowd the fruit. Most berries can be left whole (hull and slice strawberries); cherries should be pitted and stemmed; apples, pears, and stone fruit can be cored or pitted and sliced. Transfer to freezer and freeze until solid, about 4 hours. Once frozen, transfer fruit to resealable freezer bags, label, and freeze for up to 6 months.

TOASTING NUTS

To toast nuts such as almonds, pecans, and walnuts, preheat oven to 350°F. Spread nuts in a single layer on a rimmed baking sheet. Bake, tossing occasionally, until golden and fragrant, 10 to 12 minutes; start checking after 6 minutes if nuts are sliced or chopped. Pine nuts require 5 to 7 minutes. For hazelnuts, bake until skins split, 10 to 12 minutes; when cool enough to handle, rub in a clean kitchen towel to remove skins.

TOASTING COCONUT

Preheat oven to 350°F. Spread coconut in a single layer on a rimmed baking sheet. Bake until just starting to brown, tossing occasionally, 5 to 10 minutes.

ACKNOWLEDGMENTS

Thank you to the hardworking team who produced this book, our 99th!, led by Editorial Director Susanne Ruppert. Invaluable was the talented Michael McCormick, who is responsible for the beautiful design and art direction that graces these pages. Thank you to food editor Laura Rege, who brought her baking skills to the table, developing delicious recipes and offering endless insight. Special thanks also to Sarah Carey, whose love for fruit desserts is evident throughout this book.

Longtime friend of the Martha Stewart family, photographer Johnny Miller shot the mouth-watering images, while food stylist Rebecca Jurkevich, ably assisted by Cybelle Tondu, worked her culinary magic, deftly weaving piecrusts, poaching pears, and whipping cream to surreal heights. Prop stylist Sarah Smart aptly added the perfect touches to ensure everything looked as good as it tasted. Thank you to the extraordinary Caitlin Haught Brown for her meticulous and thoughtful recipe-testing notes; Kavita Thirupuvanam for her lovely mango kulfi recipe; Nanette Maxim, Laura Wallis, and Sanaë Lemoine for their dependable editorial support; and Kim Dumer and Ryan Mesina for their expertise with image rights.

Warm thanks to Kevin Sharkey for his creative guidance, and to the rest of the Marquee Brands team, particularly Thomas Joseph, Lindsay Leopold, Kimberly Miller-Olko, Stella Cicarone, Lindsey Groginski, Judy Morris, Anduin Havens, and Sophie Roche. As ever, thank you to our friends and colleagues at *Martha Stewart Living* for their continued ability to teach and inspire.

We are pleased to collaborate with our Clarkson Potter family, namely Jennifer Sit, Lydia O'Brien, Bianca Cruz, Jennifer Wang, Robert Diaz, Kim Tyner, Terry Deal, Kate Tyler, Stephanie Davis, Jana Branson, Aaron Wehner, Francis Lam, and Marysarah Quinn.

We are grateful to our loyal readers and customers, who guide everything we do.

PHOTO CREDITS

All photography credits to Johnny Miller with the following exceptions:

Sang An: Page 212
Will Anderson: Pages 27, 77
Bryan Gardner: Page 227
Gentl+Hyers:
Pages 58, 61, 70, 78, 82, 180
Randy Harris: Page 216
Raymond Hom: Page 65

John Kernick: Page 156
Mike Krautter: Pages 42, 72
Ryan Liebe: Pages 117, 118, 160
Jonathan Lovekin:
Pages 136, 199, 220
David Malosh: Pages 41, 187
Kate Mathis: Page 38
Marcus Nilsson:
Pages 23, 69, 122, 143, 147, 152, 183, 195, 211
Kana Okada: Page 46

Paola+Murray: Pages 167, 203
Con Poulos: Pages 148, 223
Linda Pugliese: Page 228
Chris Simpson: Page 168
Robin Stein: Page 98
Christopher Testani:
Pages 139, 204
Mikkel Vang: Page 155
Lennart Weibull: Page 208

INDEX